TEACHING READING AND WRITING THROUGH CHILDREN'S LITERATURE

K. Sue Bradley
Jack Bradley
Shirley Ermis

University Press of America,® Inc.
Lanham · Boulder · New York · Toronto · Oxford

Copyright © 2003 by
University Press of America,® Inc.
4501 Forbes Boulevard
Suite 200
Lanham, Maryland 20706
UPA Acquisitions Department (301) 459-3366

PO Box 317
Oxford
OX2 9RU, UK

Library of Congress Control Number: 2003109229
ISBN 0-7618-2643-2 (paperback : alk. ppr.)

CONTENTS

UNIT 1: LANGUAGE AND LITERACY
Page 1

Activity and Grade Level
20 activities

UNIT 2: PHONEMIC AWARENESS
Page 13

Activity and Grade Level
20 activities

UNIT 3: WORD RECOGNITION AND IDENTIFICATION
Page 23

Activity and Grade Level
20 activities

UNIT 4: VOCABULARY
Page 37

Activity and Grade Level
30 activities

UNIT 5: COMPREHENSION
Page 57

Activity and Grade Level
45 activities

UNIT 6: DICTIONARY/REFERENCE SKILLS
Page 85

Activity and Grade Level
20 activities

UNIT 7: COMPOSITION/WRITING MECHANICS
Page 105

Activity and Grade Level
54 activities

UNIT 8: INTERDISCIPLINARY CURRICULAR CONNECTIONS
Page 133

Activity and Grade Level
45 activities

INTRODUCTION

Teaching Reading and Writing Through Children's Literature is designed to give teachers ideas for activities they can use in their classrooms to involve students with children's literature as they guide students' learning of language arts. This text is going to be used as a supplement in introductory reading education courses for both pre-service and in-service classroom teachers. This text provides opportunities to integrate reading, writing, listening, speaking, and thinking with content areas. The activities are designed to enhance children's enjoyment and understanding of books. The enjoyment and learning possible through children's literature will contribute to children's desires to want to learn to read, read better, or do more reading.

Teaching Reading and Writing Through Children's Literature offers an array of suggestions for teachers. Teachers are encouraged to pick and choose, add to, take away from, and delete any activities in the process of tailoring this book to fit the needs of specific classrooms and individual students. Each of the lessons can be easily presented without prior training and can be used with both struggling readers and more advanced readers. This kind of flexibility allows the teacher to adapt the resources in this book to a more individualistic teaching style. It also permits more sensitive attention to the problems and possibilities of particular students.

It has been our experience that children who become involved with stories that cause them to giggle, laugh, and feel real emotions will become readers for life. It is with this end in mind that we bring this book forward as a tool to be used to bring reading and writing instruction to life and children into the world of books and wonderment.

Unit 1

Language and Literacy

U nit 1 contains an assortment of learning activities related to the development of early literacy. The purpose of these activities is to emphasize literacy behaviors that occur prior to conventional literacy. Children must "know that print represents a message and must be sensible as spoken language, and understand the concepts represented by the language used to talk about print" (Heilman, et al, 1998, p. 59). The functions, or purposes of language, will be shown in oral language and dramatic play activities, with an emphasis on understanding the concept of story and print awareness. The activities are designed to enhance children's enjoyment and understanding of books. The enjoyment and learning possible through children's literature will contribute to children's desire to learn to read.

Functions of Language

"An important aspect of learning for children is the acquisition of a wide range of language functions, to serve different purposes in various environments" (Ruddell, 2002, p. 44). Halliday in (Ruddell, 2002) identifies the following seven types of language functions:

1. "Instrumental ("I want"): satisfying material needs.

2. Regulatory ("do as I tell you"): controlling the behavior of others.

3. Interactional ("me and you"): getting along with others.

4. Personal ("here I come") identifying and expressing the self through linguistic interaction.

5. Heuristic ("tell me why"): learning and exploring both internal and external reality.

6. Imaginative ("let's pretend"): creating a world of one's own.

7. Informative ("I've got something to tell you"): communicating content and new information" (p.44).

Gail Tompkins (2001) tells us that children learn these functions of language and literacy through observing and participating in authentic real-life experiences. Children's books can provide the medium to simulate these experiences. Children learn about books and print awareness as they observe print around them, listen to read alouds and experiment with print themselves. Experiences with children's literature facilitate the learning of letter and word concepts.

1. Book orientation concepts (how to hold books, turn pages, how the words tell the story).

2. Directionality concepts (we read left to right, top to bottom, match voice to print).

3. Letter and word concepts (identify letter names, match upper and lower case letters, sentences of words, capital letter begins a sentence , notice punctuation marks, space marks the boundaries between words and sentences) (p.112).

Oral language is developed, not in isolation from, but in conjunction with, reading, and writing. Heilman, Blair, and Ripley (2002), describe the relationship between oral language and reading as being reciprocal.
"Student language awareness depends heavily on their literacy experiences, which help them to understand language features, such as syntax and semantics, and to develop their vocabularies. Direct experiences with reading and writing enhance and facilitate the development of

language awareness, which enhances and facilitates literacy and reasoning development" (p.60). Because language is the key to literacy, a language-rich environment is vital. What constitutes a language- rich environment? It is an environment that encourages literacy development by providing time, children's books and materials for language play. Language play can take many forms. Dramatic play activities can allow children to take on the role of a policeman, a firefighter, or whatever. Classroom centers can facilitate oral language development while teaching the narrative story structure. Important characteristics of predictable books that help them facilitate the development of oral language (Heilman, 2002) include:

1. They contain strong rhythm and rhyme.

2. They contain repeated language patterns.

3. They have a logical sequence.

4. They have supportive illustrations.

5. They demonstrate traditional story structure (p. 111-112).

Language and Literacy Activities

1. Telephone the Community Helper (K-2) Literacy Play Center

    A. Purpose: To develop oral language skill through role playing and dramatic play.

    B. Materials: A selection of children's books about community helpers (the fireman, the policeman, doctor, nurse, etc.)

    C. Introduction and Procedures: During a study of community helpers, the children will take turns assuming the role of a community helper and a person in need of assistance. Children will discover first-hand the importance of giving specific directions. A list of scenarios would facilitate this activity:

        • Call the fire department to report a fire.

        • Call the police to report an accident.

- Call a doctor because someone is sick and nobody is home.

2. Telephone a Character (K-2)

A. Purpose: To develop oral language skill through role playing and dramatic play.

B. Materials: A series of books by one author about the same character. Example: "Arthur" books by Marc Brown.

C. Introduction and Procedures: During the author study, the children will have been introduced to a number of books about the same character. Children like to talk. This activity capitalizes on this as children telephone the main character and discuss the plot or something related to the stories.

3. Language Experience (K-3)

A. Purpose: To develop oral language and provide practice in choral reading word by word.

B. Materials: A selection of children's books related to a specific theme like celebrations:

   I'm in Charge of Celebrations by Byrd Baylor
   Apple Pie Fourth of July by Janet Wong

C. Introduction and Procedures: Brainstorm "celebration;" word; creating a concept map as words are suggested by the children.

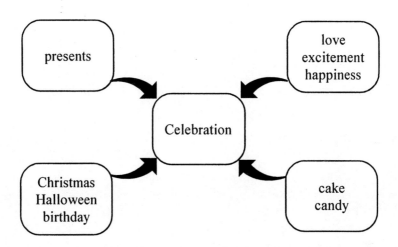

Show the different books about the celebrations. As a class, choose a celebration to write a group dictated story on chart tablet to display for re-reading throughout the unit on "celebrations."

4. Story Re-Telling (K-4)

    A. Purpose: To assist students in the understanding of plot in narrative selections.

    B. Materials: A selection of familiar stories. Fairy tales or nursery rhymes are excellent sources for this activity.

    C. Introduction and Procedures: The teacher selects one tale to read to the students and the children identify the main characters and events in the story. Then, they name the events of the story. The events can be written on sentence strips. After the events are sequenced, the children re-tell the story as a group. For young children, the events may be in pictures.

5. Let's Pretend (K-2) Literacy Play Center

    A. Purpose: To promote creativity and develop student imagination.

    B. Materials: A selection of children's books

C. Introduction and Procedures: The teacher and students will share a number of stories about young children. Then the teacher will say, "Let's pretend the characters are now all grown up. Who are they? What are their lives like? Brainstorm with students.

Jack in the Beanstalk used his riches to help the poor; became the mayor of his town; planted beanstalks across the world.

6. Puppetry (K-5)

A. Purpose: To provide opportunities for children to develop communication skills.

B. Materials: A selection of children's books, paper plates, paper bags, or other materials planned to make puppets.

C. Introduction and Procedures: Children enjoy making simple puppets and often respond to them like they are real people. Paper bag puppets require only a face to be real for children. Children are to create short riddles or dialogues using their puppets. This is fun to do in groups. Students can make mouse puppets to go with the book, *Owen*, by Kevin Henkis.

7. Dramatizing Stories (K-3)

A. Purpose: To develop oral language.

B. Materials: A selection of children's books with several characters and a short text. Familiar stories, like fairy tales, or books related to issues facing the children in the classroom.

C. Introduction and Procedures: Students listen to the story and then discuss the action. Finally the students imitate the character from the story that they choose. Minor costumes could be provided to assist the student in portraying and talking like the character.

Suggested Stories:

Frederick—Leo Lionni

The True Story of the Three Little Pigs—Jon Scieszka

The Grouchy Ladybug—Eric Carle

Hattie and the Fox—Mem Fox

Chair—Ezra Jack Keats

The Chick and the Ugly Duckling—Mirra Ginsburg

Gingerbread Boy—Paul Galdone

Ira Sleeps Over—Bernard Waber

Chrysanthemum—Kevin Henkes

Where the Wild Things Are—Maurice Sendak

The Snowy Day—Ezra Jack Keats

The Magic Fish—Freya Littledale

Tacky the Penguin—Helen Lester

The Three Little Javelinas—Susan Lowell

The Three Little Pigs—James Marshall

Brown Bear, Brown Bear—Bill Martin, Jr.

Relatives Came—Cynthia Rylant

The Elves and the Shoemaker—Freya Littledale

Amazing Grace—Mary Hoffman

Make Way for Ducklings—Robert McCloskey

The Three Little Wolves and the Big Bad Pig—Eugene Trivizas

8. Listening for Action (Grades K-2)

A. Purpose: To enhance listening skills.

B. Materials: Short Stories, paper, pencils

C. Introduction and Procedures: The teacher tells the students to listen for the action words in a passage and as it is read, write them in the order they hear them. It is important to begin with only a paragraph of a short story. Do this in short segments. Reread segments to see if the action words were identified.

9. Environmental Print/Logos (Grades K-1)

A. Purpose: To increase student awareness of the meaning of print as they see it in their environment.

B. Materials: Picture cards with logos and signs found in the community. Examples: Restaurant signs, street signs, food brands, soft drink labels, etc.

C. Introduction and Procedures: Students are shown various signs and symbols that they will see, or have seen, in the community. Students may be asked to add to the list by naming their favorite restaurants, additional signs, or favorite foods.

10. Kitchen-Literacy Play Center (Grades K-1)

A. Purpose: To allow students to develop their oral language by pretending and imitating kitchen activities.

B. Materials: Range with oven, pots, pans, eating utensils, cups, dishes, refrigerator, sink, food, magazines, food cartons, recipe cards, etc.

C. Introduction and Procedures: Students are encouraged to self-select the kitchen center and act out the activities that could happen in a kitchen. Children choose pictures from food magazines to show what they want to fix. The teacher shows how recipe cards are used and children create a card with their invented spelling or scribbles on it explaining how to fix their selected food. This can be done individually or as a group.

11. Scribbling and Journals (Grades K-1)

A. Purpose: To allow students to participate in the act of writing at the level they are capable.

B. Materials: Writing materials, pencils, crayons, paper, folders to collect student writings. C. Introduction and Procedures: The teacher could engage in language experience activities, having students share, while the teacher writes their words to be read together. Students are then encouraged to write their feelings and words. They are then given the opportunity to display and share their journals.

12. Approximations (Grades K-1)

A. Purpose: To encourage students to express their thoughts and write stories that use words that are in their oral vocabulary, yet not completely into their writing vocabulary.

B. Materials: Paper, pencils, and writing materials. Could include a computer for word processing if students are taught to use the computer for this purpose.

C. Introduction and Procedures: Students are encouraged to tell or re-tell a story. After a time of sharing, students are encouraged to write stories and then share them with the class. The teacher will encourage students to "read" what they have written. Assistance for students in recognizing words that were used in their oral and written stories they share will be provided.

13. Parts of a Book (Grades K-3)

A. Purpose: To familiarize students with the parts of books, enabling students to use them.

B. Materials: A selection of children's books that the students will be using in future activities.

C. Introduction and Procedures: Students are introduced to each part of the book, including the title page, table of contents, any information about the author, any pictures in the book.

14. Invented Spelling (K-2)

A. Purpose: To encourage students to approximate the spelling of words they have used orally and want to include in their writing.

B. Materials: Children's books to be read as a stimulus for writing.

C. Introduction and Procedures: Students are read stories; encouraged to tell and re-tell stories, and write stories of their own; to spell words the way they think they are spelled as they write stories. The teacher may have students read or tell their story in the language experience format where students' words are written down illustrating the "words written down" aspect of print. The standard spelling of words that students say during the sharing of their stories should be shared in positive ways so that students continue to use larger and more colorful words in their stories.

15. Language Experience (K-2)

A. Purpose: To help students make the connection between oral stories and written words.

B. Materials: Things brought from home to share; story books for reading aloud, sentence strips, markers.

C. Introduction and Procedures: Students are asked to bring things from home to share and discuss with the class. The teacher writes the words that the students says and then has students read the words together, reaffirming that print is words written down. Students are encouraged to share favorite stories and fond memories associated with the things that are brought to class.

16. Shared Book Experience (K-3)

A. Purpose: To encourage students to learn the conventions of print by watching and imitating the teacher as he/she reads the book.

B. Materials: Big Books for reading together with students, small copies of the books with the same title.

C. Introduction and Procedures: The teacher will demonstrate the reading of the big book, including pointing to each word as it is read. Then students are invited to join in on subsequent repeated readings of the story. Hand motions, body movement, and foot movements can be added to increase student involvement in the reading of the story.

17. Nursery Rhymes (K-1)

A. Purpose: To provide students with opportunities to have fun and enjoy language.

B. Materials: Children's book written in rhyme. C. Introduction and Procedures: Students listen to nursery rhymes and learn to repeat them by following the teacher's example. The teacher may also add movements to give the students a feeling for what is being described in the rhyme. Examples: Mary Had a Little Lamb; Jack Be Nimble; Farmer in the Dell; Peter, Peter, Pumpkin Eater, etc.

18. Folktales/Story Squares (K-3)

A. Purpose: To increase student interest in stories and help them enjoy language.

B. Materials: Children's books that are folktales.

C. Introduction and Procedures: After hearing folktales read, the student will be asked to re-tell the tales in their own words, or make up new tales. To simplify this, divide the chart board into eight squares. In each square, draw or write a clue that would help the children retell the story in sequence. Examples of folktale heroes: Pecos Bill, Paul Bunyan, Davy Crockett, Annie Oakley, Wild Bill Cody

19. Big Books (K-3)

A. Purpose: To increase student awareness of the convention of print.

B. Materials: Big Book children's books, fiction and nonfiction.

C. Introduction and Procedures: Students are focused on the book and learn the conventions of print being modeled by the teacher. After the initial reading of the book, students are invited to join in and read the book together, a number of times to help students to become familiar with the words that are needed to understand the information in the book or the story written on the pages. Students are shown that to read print, they begin on the left and go to the right; start at the top and move down, one line at a time; start on page one and move through the book, page two and then page three.

20. Office, Post Office, Library, Creative Dramatics (K-1)

A. Purpose: To increase students' oral vocabulary and help them enjoy language.

B. Materials: Office furniture, Post Office boxes and counter, minor costumes, children's books about offices, the Post Office, etc.

C. Introduction and Procedures: Students are invited to self-select a center in which they would like to pretend and imitate the action that would take place at an office, in the library, or in a familiar story. Students are allowed to be creative and make up their own words to fit the situations they might imagine.

Unit 2

Phonemic and Phonological Awareness

Phonemic and phonological awareness are also prerequisites to learning to read. Unit II will present a variety of activities which develop an awareness of sounds in spoken words. The activities are designed to meet the needs of a variety of learning styles, with a special emphasis on kinesthetic connections, a must for young learners. Research emphasizes the importance of phonemic awareness in the process of learning to read. In fact, "Phonemic awareness is more highly related to learning to read than other well-known measures such as alphabet knowledge, intelligence and listening comprehension" (Shanker, J. & Ekwall, E., 1998). Phonemic awareness can be developed through both formal and informal instruction. The crucial ingredient is experience with manipulating sounds in words. Unit II provides suggestions for both formal and informal language activities. Like phonemic awareness, alphabetic knowledge is highly correlated with later reading success (Shanker, J. & Ekwall, E., 1998). Unit II provides specific suggestions to foster the development of alphabetic knowledge.

Phonemic and Phonological
Awareness Activities

1.   Time to Rhyme (K-1)

A. Purpose: To provide students with practice in identifying rhyme in the context of a story.

B. Materials: Picture book containing rhyme; picture cards of rhyming words from story.

C. Introduction and Procedures: The teacher reads aloud from a picture book containing rhyming words. As the teacher reads the first few pages of the book he emphasizes with tone the rhyming words. The teacher instructs students to clap when they hear two words that rhyme. When students clap the teacher calls on students to state the rhyming words (example: cat and rat). The teacher than says: "I say cat . You say_____." After the reading of the story students participate in a picture sort. Picture cards consisting of the rhyming words from the story are constructed. After the teacher models how to sort the pictures into piles of rhyming words, students practice the activity in pairs or small groups.

2.   More Time to Rhyme (K-1)

A. Purpose: To provide students with practice in producing rhyme in the context of a story.

B. Materials: Big Book containing rhyme; post-it notes.

C. Introduction and Procedures: The teacher reads aloud from a Big Book containing rhyme. As the teacher reads the first few pages of the book he emphasizes with tone the rhyming words. Next, the teacher pauses at the end of phrases and lets the students supply the rhyming words. The words have been covered with post-it notes. Ater the students predict each rhyming word the post-it note is removed and students' predictions are checked. The teacher models how to select a word that not only has the same ending sound but also makes sense in the sentence. The post-it notes are once again placed on selected rhyming words. On the second reading of the Big Book, students are asked to think of other words that would also rhyme and make sense in the story. These words are written on the post-it notes. Each sentence is repeated with the new words supplied by the students to make sure they rhyme and make sense in the story.

3. What is a Sentence? (K-1)

A. Purpose: To strengthen students' awareness that sentences are made of strings of words.

B. Materials: Big Book containing repetitive language; blocks or interlocking cubes.

C. Introduction and Procedures: During the reading of a Big Book, the teacher points to each word as the book is read to reinforce the concept that individual words make up sentences. During the second reading of the book, each student is given ten blocks, which they will use to represent words in a sentence. The teacher explains to students that each block represents one word. The teacher selects a short sentence from the book. She models how to use the blocks to represent the sentence, making sure to model left to right progression and proper spacing between words. After arranging her blocks, the teacher points to each block while pronouncing the word it represents. Working in pairs and with teacher guidance the students are asked to repeat the process with their blocks. The students check their work by comparing the number of blocks they have placed before them with the actual sentence from the Big Book. The teacher selects longer sentences from the story as students become familiar with the activity.

4. Clapping and Counting Syllables (K-2)

    A. Purpose: To provide students with practice in analyzing words into syllables.

    B. Materials: Children's book containing words with varying number of syllables from one to five; pocket chart; picture cards, number cards.

    C. Introduction and Procedures: During the reading of a children's book, the teacher selects several words from the story. Picture cards representing the words from the story are placed in a hat or container. Using the top row of a pocket chart, the teacher arranges cards to display the numbers 1, 2, 3, 4, and 5 from left to right. Each student takes his turn pulling a picture card from the basket. The word is pronounced and with teacher guidance the students clap and count the number of syllables. The student then places the picture card beneath the correct number card in the pocket chart.

5. Making Words From Syllables (K-1)

    A. Purpose: To reinforce students' ability to synthesize words from their separate syllables.

    B. Materials: picture book, picture cards.

    C. Introduction and Procedures: The teacher reads a story to the class. A set of picture cards depicting familiar objects from the story is used to play the following game. The teacher holds up a picture card and says the name of the object one syllable at a time. When doing this, the teacher speaks very clearly inserting a definite pause between each syllable (example: di-no-saur). When the students figure out the word they pronounce the word normally and in a syllable-by-syllable manner.

6. I Spy Fun With Onsets and Rimes (K-1)

    A. Purpose: To reinforce students' ability to blend onsets and rimes.

B. Materials: Big Book.

C. Introduction and Procedures: During the shared reading of a Big Book, the teacher selects an object from the illustration of the book being read. The teacher tells students, "I spy something that begins with the sound /f/". There should at least two objects on the page that could be possible answers. The students, who have a guess, raise their hands and wait to be called on. Next the teacher says, "The object also ends with /ish/." Students are called on to give the correct answer. Next, students are taught a simple chant.

> I spy something that begins with /f/
>
> and it ends with /ish/.
>
> Put the sounds together
>
> and it says: fish.

7. **Puppet Fun With Phonemes (K-1)**

A. Purpose: To provide students practice with blending isolated phonemes into a word.

B. Materials: Children's picture book; puppet representing a character from the book.

C. Introduction and Procedures: As the teacher reads the picture book to students, he/she stops periodically to have students determine the next word in the story by blending phonemes and crosschecking predictions using context. The teacher presents the puppet as speaking "funny" by saying words sound-by-sound for children to figure out. The teacher, using the puppet, says:

> "/f/-/i/-/ish/…I said _____."

8. **Rubber Band Stretch (K-1)**

A. Purpose: To provide students practice with segmenting words into three or four phonemes.

B. Materials: children's picture books; large rubber band.

C. Introduction and Procedures: The teacher selects a book to read to the class in which there are numerous examples of familiar words that contain three or four phonemes. After reading the story, the teacher selects several words from the story which have three or four phonemes. The teacher models with a large rubber band how to stretch out a word as the word is pronounced:

/rrrrrrrr-/aaaaaaaa-/tttttttt/.

Next the teacher models with the stretched out band how to bring the rubber band back to its original length and say the word normally: /rat/. Students pretend to stretch rubber bands as they say the sound in different words from the book selected by the teacher.

9. **Auditory Discrimination (Grades 1-4)**

A. Purpose: To provide students with practice in hearing vowel sounds.

B. Materials: Provide a picture book, duplicated sheet similar to the one shown and pencils.

Long a	Short a	Long e	Short e	Long i	R controlled
Short i	Short o	Long o	Short u	Long u	

C. Introduction and Procedures: Begin your presentation by reading a picture book to the class. The teacher should choose some words from the book which would fall under each of the headings on the duplicated sheet. After reading the book, the teacher reads the words chosen to the class and the students must write the words under the proper headings. (With younger children, it may be necessary to do this exercise as a group on the chalkboard.)

10. Phonemic Segmentation (Grades K-1)

A. Purpose: To increase student awareness of how words are made up of sounds.

B. Materials: Index cards or 3 x 3 cards, counters such as buttons or chips, picture file.

C. Introduction and Procedures: A card, divided into three equal parts is placed before the child. The word that matches the picture is said aloud by the teacher, emphasizing the three sounds. The teacher then says the word again and places a button or chip on the card in squares as each sound is said. The student is then told to count the sounds as the teachers says the word and then as the student says the word, for practice.

O	O	. O

11. Sounds in the Context/Language Experience Activity (K-2)

A. Purpose: To increase student phonemic awareness.

B. Materials: Words selected from a story dictated to the teacher. C. Introduction and Procedures: The teacher selects words from a story dictated earlier in the day. These words are then extended into practice in counting sounds, perhaps in a game such as Phonemic Segmentation.

12. Practicing Sounds Using Alphabet Books (Grades K-1)

A. Purpose: To increase student awareness of sounds connected with the print in books.

B. Materials: Alphabet books.
C. Introduction and Procedures: Students are shown alphabet books and asked to imitate the sounds of the letters in them. The teacher

can then use the sounds to create three letter words for students to figure out.

13. Creating Letters in Art (Grades K-1)

A. Purpose: To increase student awareness of sounds.

B. Materials: Art materials, glue, scissors, paper, and pencils.

C. Introduction and Procedures: Students are shown the letter of the day and use art materials to create that letter. Final products are held up and the sounds of the letters practiced until everyone has had a turn.

14. Select the Sound (Grades K-1)

A. Purpose: To increase student awareness of beginning sounds.

B. Materials: Picture cards showing familiar objects. C. Introduction and Procedures: Students are asked to select the card with the object that begins with the sound being practiced.

15. Segmenting Beginning Sounds (Grades K-1)

A. Purpose: To increase student awareness of beginning sounds.

B. Materials: Picture cards showing familiar animals, objects, and things starting with the sounds to be practiced.

C. Introduction and Procedures: Students are shown letters and practice making the sounds. Then the picture cards are added and students are asked to tell what sound the pictures begin with. Students are finally asked to name other animals, objects, things that begin with the same sound.

16. Segmenting Ending Sounds (Grades K-1)

A. Purpose: To increase student phonemic awareness.

B. Materials: Picture cards showing familiar animals, objects, and things that end in the sounds being practiced.

C. Introduction and Procedures: Students will be shown the cards and asked to blend the sounds along with the teacher, with emphasis on the last sound. These pictures are then named quicker leading to rhyming words or names of animals, etc., with the emphasis remaining on the ending sound.

Example: bat, cat, rat.

17. Sound Matching (Grades K-1)

A. Purpose: To increase student skills in phonemic awareness, beginning sounds.

B. Materials: None.

C. Introduction and Procedures: Have students line up for lunch by beginning sounds of their first names. By the teacher making the sounds of the beginning letters of students names, student will have to match the beginning sounds of their names in order to line up for lunch correctly.

18. Blending (Grades K-1)

A. Purpose: To increase student skills in blending sounds.

B. Materials: Letters for display on a magnetic board.

C. Introduction and Procedures: Students practice saying the sounds of letters that are shown. Then students are asked to blend the sounds of two letters together, then three letters. Practice would progress from slow and exaggerated, to faster and more precise.

19. Segmenting Separate Sounds in Words (Grades K-1)

A. Purpose: To increase student phonemic awareness.

B. Materials: Enough paper squares to match the phonemes in the word being used.

C. Introduction and Procedures: As the teacher pronounces the word a square with the first sound is set before the student. As the second sound is pronounced, a second square is placed before the student in the second position going left to right. As the third sound is pronounced, the third sound is placed in the row of squares to indicate that the word has three sounds. (A square will have only one sound on it, although it may have more than one letter.

Example: b oa t would have three squares for the three sounds. Then the teacher should have students follow along as a counter or button is placed on the first square as the first sound is pronounced and then the second, and finally the third.

20. Tapping the Number of Sounds (Grades K-1)

A. Purpose: To increase student phonemic awareness.

B. Materials: Words chosen from children's books being read in the classroom.

C. Introduction and Procedures: Students will be shown one word at a time on a large word card. The teacher will say the word, emphasizing the individual sounds in the word. The teacher will then say the word emphasizing the individual sounds in the word, while tapping the sounds. Students will then be asked to join in and practice tapping the sounds heard in the word.

Unit 3

Word Recognition
and Identification

In order for students to read fluently and reach their full comprehension potential, they must develop a large number of words that they recognize instantly (word recognition) and also they must be able to use decoding strategies (word identification) to identify unfamiliar words. Students learn to identify unfamiliar words by several methods including phonic analysis, by analogy, syllabic analysis, and morphemic analysis. Phonic analysis includes using phoneme-grapheme correspondences, phonic generalizations, and spelling patterns to decode words while reading. Identifying words by analogy involves decoding by associating unknown words with words students already know. For example students use their knowledge of the work *sheep* to decode *creep*. Next, when students reach the middle grades, they learn to divide words into syllables in order to read longer multi-syllabic words such as *inconvenience* and *temporary*. Lastly, word identification strategies include morphemic analysis. Morphemic analysis includes the use of root words and affixes to identify unfamiliar words. Students remove prefixes or suffixes to identify the much easier root word first. Then they add the affixes. This strategy can be very useful with words like *transportation* and *unlikely* (Tompkins, 2003).

Word Recognition and Identification Activities

1. Sight Word Practice (Grades 2-4)

   A. Purpose: To provide practice in using small words which are not phonetically decodable.

   B. Materials: A selection of picture books, paper, and pencils.

   C. Introduction and Procedures: Give a picture book to each child. Next, write ten words on the chalkboard. These should be frequently used words which cannot be decoded phonetically. The children are to find five of these words in sentences in their books. After finding the words, they are to copy the sentence on their paper. When everyone is finished, the children should take turns reading their sentences. A sample word list follows:

to	new	walk	out	put	was	where
who	eight	into	do	you	there	of
once	what	are	your	saw	take	seven

2. Fun With Function Words (Grades K-1)

   A. Purpose: To provide practice recognizing high-frequency function words.

   B. Materials: A selection of picture books; fifty-two 3x5 colored index cards (8 different colors).

   For this activity, select picture books that contain a large percentage of high-frequency function words. Function words hold sentences together by connecting and relating meaning carrying words. Function words include prepositions (for, in), articles (the, an, a), conjunctions (and, but), pronouns (he, we), and helping verbs (could, was). Using phrases or sentences from the story and additional sentences if necessary, prepare fifty-two 3x5 index cards with a short phrase or sentence containing one function word on each card. Four cards should have the same function word, but in different sentences. Cards containing the same function word should be the same color.

C. Introduction and Procedures: During the shared reading of a Big Book, use highlighting tape to focus students attention on high-frequency function words. After the reading, students form groups of two to four children and play a game using the color-coded cards prepared by the teacher. The dealer gives each player six cards. The remaining cards are placed facedown. Students take turns asking for cards with the same color. For example, a student might say, "I would like a blue card." If another student has a blue card, that student lays the card, sentence up, on the desk. The student who requested the card then reads the face-up sentence. If the student is able to correctly read the sentence, the student keeps the card. If the player is not able to read the sentence, the card is returned to its original owner. When a student gives another student one of his cards he draws from the face down pile until all cards are distributed. When a student has four cards of the same color, the student puts all the cards on the table and reads the sentences. These cards are then placed in a discard pile. The winner is the first player to have no cards left to play.

3. Draw a Sound (Grades K-3)

A. Purpose: This is an activity to provide practice in using beginning sounds.

B. Materials: Provide a selection of picture books, a shoe box filled with letter cards, paper and pencils.

C. Introduction and Procedures: Each child is given a picture and is instructed to draw a card from the shoe box. The cards the students draw will have letters printed on them. They are to find words in their picture book beginning with the letter they each draw. At the end of a time limit, whoever has the most words wins the game. (It is important to use consonant letters which are more commonly seen in order to give everyone an equal chance.)

4. Listen For That Sound (Grades K-3)

A. Purpose: To provide practice in hearing specific consonant sounds.

B. Materials: Provide a selection of story titles, paper and pencils.

C. Introduction and Procedures: The teacher should write a letter on the chalkboard and the children should practice saying that sound. Then the children should number their papers down the left side of their paper. The teacher then says the name of the book and instructs the students to write "yes" next to number one if they hear the sound of the letter on the chalkboard. The students should not see the story title written down. If they do not hear the sound of the letter that is written on the board, they should write "no" next to number one. Repeat this exercise with all the story titles.

5. Beginning Consonant Race (Grades K-3)

A. Purpose: To provide students with repetition of beginning sounds.

B. Materials: A selection of picture books, paper and pencils.

C. Introduction and Procedures: Give each child a book. Then write a beginning consonant on the chalkboard. Make sure to give example words which begin that consonant sound. The students should then be instructed to write down any word they find which begins with the sound on the chalkboard. Set a time limit on this activity. The student who has the most words written down with the correct sound at the end of the time limit wins the game. Variation: Use consonant blends, such as cl, bl, cr, or br, or consonant digraphs, such as sh, th, wh, or ch, instead of beginning consonant sounds.

6. Build a Word (Grades K-3)

A. Purpose: To provide students with practice in word recognition.

B. Materials: Poster board cut into one inch squares with letters printed on them and a selection of picture books.

C. Introduction and Procedures: Give each child fifteen of the one inch squares, five with vowels and ten with consonants. Also give each child a picture book. The students are to use their squares to form words in their picture book. After a set time limit, the student who has used the most letters correctly wins the game.

7. Long and Short Vowels (Grades 1-4)

A. Purpose: To give children practice in reading words with long and short vowel sounds.

B. Materials: A selection of picture books, paper, and pencils.

C. Introduction and Procedures: Instruct the children to write down all the one syllable words that they can find in their books. The books should be picture books with only a small amount of writing. When the students complete this, have them underline short vowel one syllable words with a blue crayon and long vowel one syllable words with a red crayon. Repeat this exercise by having the children trade books with someone. Have them compare their answers.

8. Vowel Discrimination (Grades 2-4)

A. Purpose: To provide students with practice in using vowels.

B. Materials: Strips of paper, a selection of picture books, pencils, and a prepared duplicated sheet.

C. Introduction and Procedures: Give each child a picture book and instruct the students to find words with the same vowel sound as on the duplicated sheet. The first child to cover all the boxes with words to match the vowel sounds wins the game. Repeat this exercise for additional practice for the students.

hat	nut	go	bet	hot
far	turn	word	cup	game
kite	goat	gate	her	hit
meet	box	cute	fir	cat

9. R-Controlled Vowel Sound Cover Up (Grades 2-4)

A. Purpose: To provide students with practice in identifying r-controlled vowel sounds.

B. Materials: A selection of picture books, strips of paper, pencils and set of cards using vowel sounds with r-controlled vowel sounds (er, ir, or, ur). See example below:

er	ir	ur
ur	er	or
ur	ir	or

C. Introduction and Procedures: Tell each student to select a partner. Every child has a picture book, but two children share a card such as the one shown. When the teacher says "go", the children will look for words with the r-controlled vowel, write them on strips of paper and cover the appropriate box on the card (As is done in Bingo). The first group that covers its card wins the game. They must read the words aloud to the class before they officially are proclaimed to be the winners. Repeat this game for extra practice. Example words with r-controlled vowels are as follows:

burn	word	bird	her
turn	work	fir	serve
curve	worm	first	nerve

10. Leave Out a Letter (Grades 3-5)

A. Purpose: To give students practice in recognizing partially completed words.

B. Materials: A selection of picture books, paper, pencils, and 3x5 cards.

C. Introduction and Procedures: Provide a book and a 3x5 card for each student. The student is to write ten words on the card, leaving out one letter in each word (Example: Hap _ y). After writing out the words, the student is to trade cards with someone and then try to fill in the letter to complete the words on that card. The student may use the book if necessary. This activity can be made more difficult by leaving out more than one letter in each word.

11. Blend Wagon Train (Grades 2-5)

A. Purpose: To associate letter blends with their corresponding sounds.

B. Materials: Duplicated pictures of a wagon for each child, a selection of picture books, paper and pencils. Each wagon should have a blend written on it before the pictures are given to the children.

C. Introduction and Procedures: Give each student a picture of a wagon similar to the one shown. The students are to use a book to locate words with the blend they have on their wagon. After finding such words, they are to write them on their wagon. At the end of a specified time period, whoever has the most words with their blend wins the race. At the end of the game, the students select a partner and read their words to each other. A list of blends follow:

bl	cl	fl	gl	pl	sl
br	cr	dr	fr	gr	pr
sk	sm	sc	sn	sp	st
scr	spl	spr	shr	thr	str

Variation: The same game could be played using any of the following final consonant blends.

ct	ft	ld	lf	lm	pt
nt	nk	nd	mp	lp	lt
rm	rl	rd	rk	sk	sp st

12. Substitution of Letters (Grades 2-5)

A. Purpose: To provide practice in using consonants and to improve the students' comprehension of sentences.

B. Materials: Provide paper, pencils and a selection of picture books with a limited amount of text in them.

C. Introduction and Procedures: The teacher is to read the first sentence of a picture book, changing one word in the sentence by changing a beginning consonant sound. Example: Tommy did not <u>b</u>ike to clean his room. The children are to identify the incorrect word and fix it. After going through the book, have students select a partner and follow the same procedure. The two children are to take turns changing a sentence and calling on their partners to fix it.

13. Guess Me (Grade K-9)

A. Purpose: To motivate interest in a particular book and give students practice with making words.

B. Materials: Prepared duplicated copies of the game.

C. Introduction and Procedures: Instruct the students to figure out the name of the book, or a character in the book, by working out the letter puzzle on the line provided.

My first letter is in boy, but not in Bob _____

My second letter is in due, and also in see _____

My third is in run, but not in sun _____

My fourth is in sit and also in not _____

My fifth is in call but not in cat _____

My sixth is in gave, and also in lone _____

My first is in toy, but not in boy _____

My second is in ham and also in hit _____

My third is in he, but not in ho _____

My first is in pit, but not in pig _____

My second is in gun, but on in gone _____

My third is in try, and also in car _____

My fourth is in rat, but not in ran _____

My fifth is in all and also in tell _____

My last is in eat, but not in at _____

Answer: Yertle the Turtle

14. Syllables (Grades 2-4)

A. Purpose: To identify the number of syllables contained in different words.

B. Materials: A prepared worksheet similar to the following.

C. Introduction and Procedures: Give each child a picture book and a copy of the prepared duplicated sheet. The children are to locate words with one, two, three, and four syllables and write them under the proper headings on the duplicated sheet. A time limit should be set. Whoever has the most words correctly placed at the end of the set time limit wins the game. The children should take turns reading some of their words and clapping out the syllables with the class.

How Many Syllables?

1	2	3	4

15. More Syllables (Grades 2-4)

A. Purpose: To identify one, two, and three syllable words.

B. Materials: Provide a selection of picture books, paper and pencils.

C. Introduction and Procedures: Give each student a book. Next instruct them to list all of the one syllable words from the first page of the story, the two syllable words from the second page and the three syllable words from the third. After completing this, have them trade books with another student. The same procedure should be followed with the new book. When this has been completed, the students are to compare papers.

16. Word Endings (Grades 2-4)

A. Purpose: To provide the students with practice in using suffixes.

B. Materials: A selection of picture books, paper and pencils.

C. Introduction and Procedures: The teacher should discuss endings which are added to verbs. Some examples of these are: ful, ing, less, er, ed, s, and est. The class is divided into five groups. Each child is given a picture book. Each child is to find a "doing" word and write it on the top of a sheet of paper. Then the students of one group trade papers with the students of another group and complete the following exercise. Each student should add any endings which can be used with the word they are given. Not all of the endings can be used with every word. After finishing this, each child should read his/her list of words to the class. It may be helpful to write the following example on the board.

    Jump

    Jumps

    Jumping

    Jumped

    Jumper

17. Prefixes and Suffixes (Grades 2-4)

A. Purpose: To provide practice in using prefixes and suffixes.

B. Materials: Provide a list of prefixes and suffixes, paper, pencils, and picture books.

C. Introduction and Procedures: Select some picture books that have text containing words with prefixes and suffixes. Next write a list of prefixes and suffixes on the chalkboard. Refer to the following sample list:

re-	sub-	-able	-est
dis-	pre-	-er	-ship
un-	pro-	-ful	-or
in-		-ic	-ness
con-		-ish	-ment
mis-		-ist	-less

After preparing the chalkboard, give each child a book and instruct the class to write down five words from their books that contain these prefixes and suffixes. They are to write the word in isolation, then copy the sentence as it appears in the story, and finally, write an original sentence using the word.

18. Contractions (Grades 2-5)

A. Purpose: To match contractions to their corresponding words.

B. Materials: A selection of picture books, pencils and paper.

C. Introduction and Procedures: Each child should be given a picture book and instructed to locate some contractions or their corresponding words in his book. (A child can use either do not or don't.) They are to write these words on their paper with the corresponding contraction or group of words next to it. A time limit should be set. The student with the most contractions with their corresponding words at the end of the time limit wins the game. A wall chart showing common contractions could be used to complete this activity.

19. Memory Game (Grades K-5)

A. Purpose: To increase students' word recognition.

B. Materials: Word cards containing words that need to be recognized, two for each word.

C. Introduction and Procedures: Students place the word cards face down on the table, spaced out in rows and columns. Students are to turn one card over and say the word and the try to locate the other card with the same word. If the student turns over both of the word cards with the same word, the student says the word and picks up both cards and stacks them in his/her pile. The game continues until all of the pairs of word cards have been matched. The student with the most cards is the winner.

20. Word Spy (Grades 2-5)

A. Purpose: To increase students' rapid word recognition.

B. Materials: A selection of children's books, including poetry books, high frequency vocabulary wordlist.

C. Introduction and Procedures: After students have learned to recognize a word, students are given a variety of books to look through to find the word(s) they have just learned, and then read the sentences and phrases in which the words were found. Students should be given time to find the words in a variety of meaningful contexts.

Unit 4

Vocabulary

Research and practice stress that vocabulary is a critical part of reading comprehension and content learning. Much research has been conducted that clearly describes the relationship between knowledge of vocabulary and students' ability to understand what they read. In fact, the number of difficult words in a text is the strongest predictor of text difficulty and a reader's vocabulary knowledge is the best predictor of that reader's reading level (Anderson & Freebody, 1981). This is not a hard idea to sell since it also seams to make common sense; one cannot understand text without knowing the meaning of most of the words. This relationship between vocabulary and comprehension is especially strong when reading content area text, or nonfiction, where certain words and concepts may be central to understanding a whole topic.

Much of the vocabulary instruction widely practiced in schools today has not shown to improve reading comprehension. According to Nagy (1988), most of the techniques used to teach vocabulary fail to produce in-depth word knowledge and thus do not result in increased comprehension. In order to be effective, Nagy further explains, vocabulary instruction must provide both adequate definitions and illustrations of how words are used in natural sounding contexts. Vocabulary instruction also, to be most effective, should integrate the words taught with other knowledge, provide children with many encounters with the targeted words, and keep students actively involved. It is no wonder then that the common practice of teaching vocabulary by having students look up unknown words in a dictionary, write the definitions, memorize the definitions, and match words to definitions at the end of the week on a text is not increasing comprehension.

The vocabulary activities included in Unit IV all start with the reading of a piece of quality children's literature. Therefore, children will first encounter the new words in context. To provide greater depth of understanding the words are then "pulled" from the text to allow more in-depth study which may include definitions but certainly do not stop there. Students are actively involved with each of these activities.

Vocabulary Activities

1. **Using Describing Words (Grades 1-5)**

    A. Purpose: To expand students' vocabulary through the use of adjectives.

    B. Materials: A picture book. C. Introduction and Procedures: The teacher will read a picture book to the students. A picture book should be selected which has several very well developed characters, with different character traits. The teacher will write the character's names on the chalkboard and the students will try to come up with words which describe the different characters. The teacher will write the describing words under the proper headings on the chalkboard similar to the following (from *Hansel and Gretel*).

Hansel	Gretel	Stepmother	Father	Witch
shy	shy	mean	weak	wicked
quiet	quiet	horrible	kind	terrible
helpful	afraid	ugly	ugly	
timid				

2. Draw a Word (Grades K-4)

A. Purpose: To develop vocabulary.

B. Materials: A selection of picture books, paper, pencils, a shoe box and 3x5 cards.

C. Introduction and Procedures: Each student should be given a book and three 3x5 cards. The students are instructed to think of the words in the story which name something. Write one naming word (noun) on each card. Put the cards in the shoe box and let each child draw one. The children are to illustrate the word and write the word below the picture. After everyone is finished, share the pictures with the class.

3. Vocabulary Practice (Grades 1-3)

A. Purpose: To learn categorizing and to enrich vocabulary.

B. Materials: A picture book.

C. Introduction and Procedures: The teacher reads a picture book to the class, stopping at the end of each page to discuss specific vocabulary. Two headings should be written on the board that say, "Someone may feel," and "Someone may use." Example (based on, *Fly High, Fly Low*, by Don Freeman)

Someone may feel	Someone may use
proud	cable car
warm	building
cozy	paper sack
kind	bridge
terrible	traffic signal
gentle	umbrella
lucky	shop

As children give their responses, the teacher writes them under the appropriate category.

4. Vocabulary in Context (Grades 4-5)

    A. Purpose: To develop vocabulary.

    B. Materials: A selection of non-fiction books, paper and pencils.

    C. Introduction and Procedures: Each student should be given a book and instructed to find five words in the book which they don't know. They are to write five words on a piece of paper. For each word they must: 1. Copy the sentence from the non-fiction text where each word appears. 2. Write the dictionary definition that matches the meaning of the word as used in the non-fiction book. 3. Write an original sentence using the word.

5. Vocabulary Enrichment (Grades 3-6)

    A. Purpose: To enrich vocabulary.

    B. Materials: A variety of books.

    C. Introduction and Procedures: The teacher should prepare a list of vocabulary words, using action words and descriptive words. After the lists have been prepared, the students are asked to choose three vocabulary words. They are to find one book which relates to each of their vocabulary words. For example, using the vocabulary word "exciting," a student might choose the book, "Swiss Family Robinson." In class discussion, the students are to tell how the book relates to the word. Using short stories, rather than books might be more successful with older students. A sample word list follows. The word lists can be changed to fit any grade level.

exciting	boring	happy	hurry
interesting	sad	thrilling	love
beautiful	ugly	sleek	hate
tremendous	babbly	laugh	funny
unbelievable	awful	listen	compete
camp	discover	explore	cry
sing	run	study	

(Notice the mixture of verbs and adjectives)

6. Synonyms and Antonyms (Grades 2-5)

A. To enrich vocabulary by practice with synonyms and antonyms.

B. Materials: A prepared duplicated sheet with the titles of books on it and a pencil.

C. Introduction and Procedures: The students should be instructed to write one synonym and one antonym for each underlined word. A sample duplicated sheet is shown:

	Synonym	Antonym
The <u>Boy</u> Who Tried to Cheat Death	lad	girl
You Will Live <u>Under</u> the Sea	below	above
The <u>Funny</u> Thing	amusing	sad
Mr. Charlie, the Fireman's <u>Friend</u>	pal	enemy
Short and <u>Tall</u>	big	short
The Boy Who <u>Fooled</u> the Giant	tricked	helped

7. Antonyms (Grades 2-5)

A. Purpose: To increase vocabulary knowledge by practice in using antonyms.

B. Materials: A selection of picture books, paper, and pencils.

C. Introduction and Procedures: Each child should be given a picture book and instructed to write down ten words which describe something. Each child selects a partner and trades word lists with him/her. The students are to write opposites for each of their partner's words. When everyone is finished, the children should take turns reading some of their words with their opposites.

8. Vocabulary Log (Grades 3 and up)

A. Purpose: To increase students' vocabulary by using an individualized reading approach.

B. Materials: Quality literature and spiral notebook for each student.

C. Introduction and Procedures: During sustained silent reading, students are instructed to keep a vocabulary log. The teacher models how to construct the log by demonstrating how to select words, indicate the page number where found, and write a definition and the sentence from the text containing the selected word. The teacher shows students ways they can personalize their logs, for example by illustrating the meaning of a word.

Name *Jackie* Book *The Ghost of Panna Maria by Rita Kerr*			
word	page	definition and sentence	illustration
peered	*2*	*looked* *He stepped to the door and peered nervously inside, aware of the danger that waited for him there.*	
laugh	*7*	*Chuckled* *Her father laughed softly.*	

9. **Word Mapping (Grades 2-5)**

   A. Purpose: To expand students' vocabularies by having students study the distinguishing features of a word.

   B. Materials: Children's literature.

   C. Introduction and Procedures: The teacher will read a picture book to students and select a concept to analyze in detail using a word map. With teacher guidance students select a synonym, antonym, an example of the correct use of the word, and a non-example of use of the word. An example of a word map for the word "jubilant" is shown below.

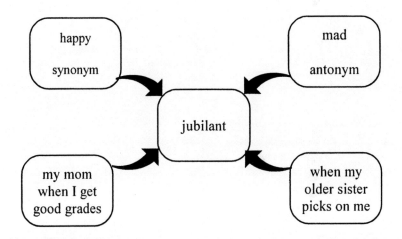

10. **Enhancing Vocabulary Through Character Mapping (Grades K-8)**

   A. Purpose: To expand students' vocabulary through an examination of character traits.

   B. Materials: Children's literature.

   C. Introduction and Procedures: The activity focuses on the possible words to describe characters, which are then supported by events and illustrations in the story. Character mapping is a way of graphically displaying words that describe characters and makes word relationships apparent. With teacher scaffolding students construct the map during and after reading. A map for *The Ghost of Panna Maria* (1990), by Rita Kerr, is shown below.

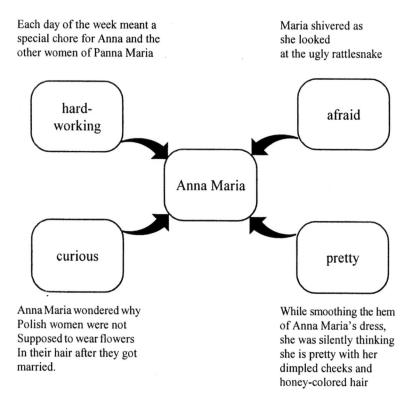

Each day of the week meant a
special chore for Anna and the
other women of Panna Maria

Maria shivered as
she looked
at the ugly rattlesnake

hard-working

afraid

Anna Maria

curious

pretty

Anna Maria wondered why
Polish women were not
Supposed to wear flowers
In their hair after they got
married.

While smoothing the hem
of Anna Maria's dress,
she was silently thinking
she is pretty with her
dimpled cheeks and
honey-colored hair

11. Characterization and Feeling Words (Grades 3-8)

A. Purpose: To provide experiences for students to perceive how an author uses vocabulary to make a character come alive.

B. Materials: A selection of children's books.

C. Introduction and Procedures: The teacher should write some feeling words on the board. These words will vary, depending on the age and literacy level of the students. Examples include:

angry	sad	worried	disgusted
excited	lonely	shy	delighted
happy	upset	nervous	embarrassed

The students are instructed to find sentences or phrases in their story that the author has used to describe feelings. The students are instructed to divide their paper as follows:

sentence	feeling
"I can't stand this anymore."	anger

12. Using Sensory Images (Grades 3-8)

A. Purpose: To develop vocabulary through the classification and connection of known ideas with unfamiliar concepts.

B. Materials: A selection of children's books, chart paper and pencils.

C. Introduction and Procedures: This activity is teacher directed with primary children. The older students are instructed to read their book specifically looking for words that provide sensory impressions. Students work in heterogeneous groups of four to complete this task to enable students of all academic levels to participate. They divide the chart paper into four sections as follows:

Touch	*Taste*	*Smell*	*Sight*	*Hearing*
smooth	sour	fragrant	bright	quiet
rough	sweet	spicy	dim	loud
gritty	bitter	smoky	glittery	faint

Sensory words are placed in the appropriate columns as they are found. Debriefing as a class offers multiple opportunities for learning new words.

13. Could it Happen? (Grades 1-4)

A. Purpose: To distinguish between fact and fancy.

B. Materials: A picture book, paper and pencils.

C. Introduction and Procedures: The children should number their papers down the left side of the page. The teacher then reads a sentence from a picture book. The children are to write "yes" if it could happen, or "no" if it could not happen. Discuss the sentences in class.

14. Concept Attainment (Grades 2-8)

A. Purpose: To expand students' understanding of unfamiliar concepts.

B. Materials: A children's book.

C. Introduction and Procedures: After reading a children's book, teacher selects at least one concept from the book that is unfamiliar to students. With teacher guidance, students complete the organizer below. The teacher begins by presenting labeled examples. Students compare the attributes in positive and negative examples. They then generate and test hypotheses. With teacher guidance, students state a definition according to the essential attributes. The teacher presents additional examples and students identify examples as "yes" or "no". Teacher confirms hypotheses, names concept, and restates definition according to essential attributes. Students generate additional examples. Students analyze thinking strategies by describing thoughts, discussing role of hypotheses and attributes, and discussing type and number of hypotheses.

```
┌─────────────────────────┐
│     Concept Name        │
│       Shelter           │
└─────────────────────────┘
```

┌──┐
│ Definition including critical attributes. The place where one │
│ lives. Protects from weather and other kinds of danger. │
└──┘

Positive examples:		Negative Examples:	
house	igloo	Umbrella	street
pueblo	apartment	doorway	raincoat
tent	houseboat	weapon	alarm
cave	hacienda	clothing	
hut	tree-house		

15. Using Context Clues (Grades 3-8)

A. Purpose: To teach the use of context clues to aid in determining word meaning.

B. Materials: A children's book.

C. Introduction and Procedures: After or during the reading of a children's book, use the following process to teach students how to use context clues to determine the meaning of an unfamiliar word. First write one sentence from the book that contains the unfamiliar word on the chalkboard or overhead projector. Underline the word and discuss the possible meaning of the word with students. Next write a second sentence on the chalkboard taken from context and discuss further. After that, the teacher asks a question or two that requires students to apply the meaning of the unfamiliar word in order to answer the question. Lastly, the students are asked to use the word in meaningful sentences.

Example

Step 1: (Sentence from text):
Princess Sarah looked very <u>elegant</u> as she entered the ballroom.

Step 2: (Second sentence from text):
In order to look <u>elegant</u> for the occasion, Princess Sarah ordered her maids to sew her a beautiful silk dress.

Step 3: (Question):
Would looking elegant be a good or bad thing?
What qualities would be associated with the word elegant?

Step 4: (Students use word to create new sentences):

---

16. Visual Imaging (Grades 1-5)

A. Purpose: To increase vocabulary knowledge by using students' tactile and kinesthetic strengths.

B. Materials: A picture book.

C. Introduction and Procedures: The teacher reads a picture book to the class, stopping at the end of each page to discuss specific vocabulary. Three headings should be written on the board that say, "New Word", "Definition", and "Motor Meaning." A definition for each new vocabulary word is obtained from a dictionary, discussed, and inserted under the appropriate column. Next, students are asked to think of a gesture that would remind them of the definition of each word. Students show their gesture to the class and the class decides on one gesture that will be used for each word. Students practice the gestures and discuss how they can aid in remembering the definition of each new vocabulary word.

See example below:

New Word	Definition	Motor Meaning
domicile	place where one lives	hands meeting over the head in a triangular "roof shape"
despair	great sadness	hands over the eyes head slanted forward

17. Vocabulary Cards (Grades 2-5)

A. Purpose: To develop vocabulary.

B. Materials: Children's books.

C. Introduction and Procedures: Select unfamiliar vocabulary from children's books students are reading. Have students write the word they want to learn on the front of an index card. On the back of the card, write these two things: 1) the definition of the word, and 2) a sentence using the word. Students use the cards to practice and test themselves. See example below:

Side One   Side Two

Bovine	—of a cow or cow-like Cowboys learn early the characteristics of a <u>bovine</u>.

18. Fun With Alliteration (Grades 3-5)

A. Purpose: to develop vocabulary

B. Materials: children's books

C. Introduction and Procedures: Before or during the reading of a children's book, select new vocabulary words important to the meaning of the text. Using the vocabulary words, have students work in groups to create sentences using the vocabulary word with alliteration. Next they draw simple illustrations for their sentences.

Example: The <u>freaky</u> frog found five funny fireflies.

19. Analyzing Features of Words (Grades 2-8)

A. Purpose: To develop concept vocabulary.

B. Materials: A children's book.

C. Introduction and Procedures: After or during the reading of a children's book, select a concept from the book that is critical to the comprehension of the text. List words in the same category in a column in a matrix. Next list in rows in the matrix, attributes or features of the category of words. Determine through interaction with the students, which words do or do not possess those features, marking in (+) and minuses (-). Lastly, discuss how the words are semantically related. See example below.

Classroom Feature Analysis for the Concept of Pets

Features

Pets	paws	fur	four legs	whiskers	meows	tail	feathers	scales	gills
Kitten	+	+	+	+	+	+	-	-	-
Dog	+	+	+	+	-	+	-	-	-
Parakeet	-	-	-	-	-	+	+	-	-
Snake	-	-	-	-	-	+	-	+	-
Goldfish	-	-	-	-	-	+	-	+	+

20. Synonym Snowflakes (Grades 1-3)

A. Purpose: To develop vocabulary

B. Materials: Children's books.

C. Introduction and Procedures: Before or during the reading of children's books, select new vocabulary concepts important to the meaning of the texts. On a bulletin board, make a winter scene. The students will make synonym snowflakes and add them to the bulletin board. In the center of the snowflake, the student will write the vocabulary word. On the snowflake points surrounding the center, the student will list as many synonyms for the word as possible.

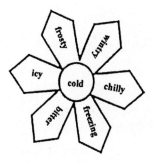

21. Graphic Organizers (Grades 2-5)

A. Purpose: To enable students to use charts and diagrams to organize information.

B. Materials: Large chart paper or poster board for drawing the graphic organizers.

C. Introduction and Procedures: Chose a graphic organizer to be used, whether it is a semantic map, a pictorial map, or other device that shows information in a graphic manner. Have students brainstorm the items that are to be written in the circles, spaces, etc. to complete the graphic organizer. Discuss the completed organizer and ask for further input.

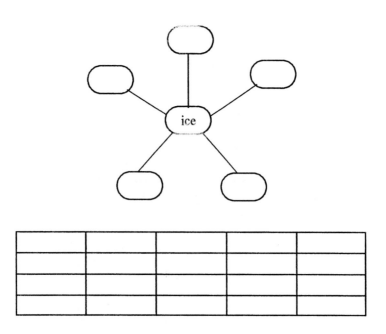

22. Semantic Mapping (Grades 2-5)

A. Purpose: To display and organize information graphically for students.

B. Materials: Chalk and chalkboard for drawing the map.

C. Introduction and Procedures: Introduce the concept and put it in a circle at the center of the chalkboard. Brainstorm with students ideas they associate with the concept. Group the words in categories, discussing why the word go together. Create a large class map that can be added to and discuss it. Extend the map as discussion continues.

23. Semantic Association (Grades 2-8)

A. Purpose: To increase students' vocabulary.

B. Materials: children's books, thesaurus.

C. Introduction and Procedures: After the reading of a children's book, divide the class into two groups, giving each group a critical vocabulary word from the story to brainstorm. Write the words on the board. Create sentences using different combinations of words. (This is fun to do orally as well as part of a written assignment. This is an excellent activity to use in guiding students to use a thesaurus.

Example: Sadako's friends wanted to <u>build</u> a <u>monument</u> to her and all the children who were killed by the bomb.

Group 1	Group 2
<u>build</u>	<u>monument</u>
make	memorial
construct	shrine
shape	statue
erect	
mold	
assemble	

24. Modified CLOZE Passages (Grades 2-5)

A. Purpose: To increase student use of context clues.

B. Materials: Stories or passages that have words deleted.

C. Introduction and Procedures: A reading passage is prepared with a few words deleted to begin with and then with more words deleted to see if students can figure out what the passage is about with more and more of the words deleted.

25. Hink Pinks (Grades 2-5)

A. Purpose: To increase students' skills in vocabulary.

B. Materials: Hink Pink examples; sample illustrations of Hink Pinks.

C. Introduction and Procedures: Students will be shown numerous examples of Hink Pinks and asked to tell what the illustrations would look like. Students will then be asked to create their own Hink Pinks and illustrate them.

Examples: sad dad, bee tree, flat mat, fat cat

Students develop clues to lead other students into their Hink Pink. An unhappy father = sad dad.   An overweight feline = fat cat.

26. Word of the Day (Grades 2-8)

A. Purpose: To increase students' vocabulary.

B. Materials: Selected words that are useful and interesting.

C. Introduction and Procedures: A new word is chosen and presented at the beginning of the day. The word may be tied to the time of the year or some special event. Have students try to guess the meaning of the word. Provide the history of the word and discuss the importance of the word. Encourage students to collect examples of the word's use.

27. Predict-O-Gram (Grades 2-8)

A. Purpose: To increase students' skills in predicting word meaning.

B. Materials: Key words from the story chosen by the teacher.

C   Introduction and Procedures: Students are given a list of key words from a story and asked to predict how the words are used in the story. Which words are used to describe the setting, characters, the story problem, the plot, or the resolution. This activity forces students to think about new vocabulary words in terms of the new story. After the story has been read, the students then discuss their predictions in terms of the actual content and structure of the story.

28. Vocabulary Self-Selection (Grades 2-8)

A. Purpose: To increase the personalization of student vocabulary learning.

B. Materials: Journals or vocabulary notebooks. C. Introduction and Procedures: Students are asked to select words from the text that are important enough for the whole class to study. Words are discussed to see what students think the meaning of the word is using the sentence and context. Definitions and pronunciations are checked. The teacher models the use of context and the use of the dictionary. Words selected are recorded in journals or vocabulary notebooks. Students should become more word conscious as they select words for the whole class to study.

29. Word Sorts (Grades 2-8)

A. Purpose: To engage students in word study.

B. Materials: Word bank collected by each student.

C. Introduction and Procedures: Each student looks at his/her word bank and groups words together in some way. The student then shows the words they grouped and asks another student to guess how the words are alike. Students are then asked to tell how they grouped their words, how they are alike.

30. Contextual Redefinition (Grades 3-8)

A. Purpose: To increase students' understanding of the hard words in a passage being read.

B. Materials: Words chosen as important words for the understanding of the passage being read.

C. Introduction and Procedures: Words are chosen that are important to the understanding of the passage, which may pose a problem for students. These words are listed on the chalkboard or the overhead. Students are asked to come to agreement on what they think the words mean. The words are then presented in context by writing the sentences. Students are asked to look at the context and see if they can tell what the words mean. Finally, the words are looked up in the dictionary and the group chooses the most appropriate definition.

Unit 5

Comprehension Skills

Traditionally, reading comprehension has been viewed as a set of skills that students have to master, which would result in a synthesis of skills. Unit V contains a variety of activities that require students to use background knowledge, text cues and contextual information to construct meaning. Focuses are on both literal and inferential meaning. In addition, to become successful critical thinkers, students have to have experiences in analyzing and evaluating information. The lessons deal with the use of both narrative and informational texts. Specific reading skills are addressed, but they are embedded into literature-based activities. For example, in one lesson, the teacher places the titles of a random selection of books in a grab bag. Without looking at the titles, students "grab" a card from the bag. They are then directed to write the story that goes with the title. When the children are finished writing their stories, they are given the corresponding book to read. This activity develops inferencing skills within the context of real literature. "Motivation must be at the heart of the language arts curriculum because the quality of the content of the program matters little if it is students" (Graves, 2001, p.259). The activities included in Unit V are designed to pique student interest through hands-on experiences, active student participation and drama. Activities focus on using prior knowledge, asking and answering questions, creating mental images and monitoring comprehension.

Comprehension Activities

1. Figurative Language (Grades 2-8)

A. Purpose: To raise the level of student understanding of figurative language.

B. Materials: A selection of children's books containing similes, metaphors, personification, allusion, hyperbole, exaggeration, or whatever element(s) you plan to student.

C. Introduction and Procedures: To introduce the idea of figurative language, give students several examples of the specific types of figurative language. Examples: What do the following mean?

1. Gossip is a knife that cuts friendships apart. (metaphor)

2. The puppy was as white as snow. (simile)

3. The night sang sweet songs to us as we slept. (personification)

4. The ruby is as read as blood. (simile)

5. You bought enough food to feed an army. (exaggeration)

6. Tom is growing like a weed. (simile)

7. When money became missing from the bank, the teller became Sherlock Holmes. (allusion)

You would select the kinds of figurative language based on the age and ability of your students. Students brainstorm additional examples of the types of figurative language under study. These are written on the board. Students scan children's books for additional examples to add to the list.

2. Author's Purpose (Grades 4-8)

A. Purpose: To develop student understanding of the author's purpose in writing something.

B. Materials: A wide variety of books including fiction, non-fiction, biography, an encyclopedia, a joke book, etc.

C. Introduction and Procedures: Discuss the meaning of the words inform, criticize, entertain, persuade, and ask students to give examples of something they might read that fit each of these categories. Read the beginning of a biography... Abraham Lincoln was elected President of the United States in 1860. Ask questions regarding its type. Read the beginning of another para-graph...Casey's poor batting caused us to lose. He has no excuse. Ask questions regarding its type. Read a joke from a joke book. Follow the same procedure. Have students work in groups looking for indications of the authors purpose in specific paragraphs. Emphasize that an author can display more than one in a book.

3. **Point of View (Grades 4-8)**

    Point of View refers to the way a story is told. Writers use three different methods.

    1. first person

    2. third person

    3. omniscient

    A. Purpose: To promote reading comprehension by developing student understanding of the author's use of Point of View.

    B. Materials: A selection of children's books, some written from each of the three points of view.

    C. Introduction and Procedures: Explain the three points of view by giving examples:

        1. He wanted to go but decided it was too late (third person).

        2. I was really excited when they started singing "Happy Birthday" (first person).

3. She had not known what would happen if she went through that door. (omniscient)

Have students look at their books and make a prediction as to the author's Point of View. Complete the following graphic on the board:

First Person	Third Person	Omniscient

This activity stimulates student interest in reading the text.

4. **Reading and Understanding Graphs (Grades 2-8)**

    A. Purpose: To have students practice comprehension of text on graphs.

    B. Materials: A selection of children's books.

    C. Introduction and Procedures: Read a short story or children's book to the group. Develop an idea for a graph related to the story read. For example: If the book told of the life expectancy of specific animals, the graph would show that information. The types of graphs used will depend on the age of the student (bar graph, circle graph, pictograph, line graph, etc.). For older or more advanced students—have students create a graph related to a different book. Students then present the graphs and have students discuss and explain the information shown the graphs.

5. **You be the Teacher (Grades 3-8)**

    A. Purpose: To enhance reading comprehension

    B. Materials: A selection of children's books or short stories.

C. Introduction and Procedures: Two to four students are instructed to read the same story. After reading the story, they are to write five questions beginning with who, what, where, when, why, or how. The student who writes the question is to record the page number where the answer to the question is found. After this is done, the students ask each other their questions. If no one can answer, the questioner says, "Read page ___ to find the answer to the question." This is done until all questions have been answered.

6. **Question/Response Relationships (Grades 3-8)**

A. Purpose: To provide experiences for students to increase their reading comprehension.

B. Materials: A selection of children's books.

C. Introduction and Procedures: The teacher should develop questions to use to assist students in deciding where the answers can be found. The students are guided through deciding whether the answer is found by looking within the text, by thinking and searching, by the author and reader working together, or by using my head.

Within the Text	By Thinking & Searching	Between the Author and Reader	Use My Head

7. **Use the Context "Beep" (Grades 2-8)**

A. Purpose: To provide the student with practice in using context to figure out the meaning of an unfamiliar word.

B. Materials: A selection of children's books, 3x5 cards, dictionaries (primary dictionaries for the lower grades).

C. Introduction and Procedures: Students are directed to find five sentences in their books which contain an unfamiliar word. They are to copy each sentence on a 3x5 card, leaving out the unfamiliar word. The unfamiliar word and its definition are written on the back of the same card. Instead of writing the unfamiliar word on the front, the student writes the word "Beep." The student reads the sentence, inserting the work "Beep." The class must determine the meaning of the "Beep" in the sentence. When this is completed, the unfamiliar word and the dictionary definition are shared with the class. The class can keep a record of these unfamiliar words.

8. Author Study (Grades 3-8)

A. Purpose: To provide students with practice in critical thinking while studying a particular author's work.

B. Materials: A selection of books or short stories by the same author. (Eve Bunting, Chris Van Allsburg, etc.)

C. Introduction and Procedures: Students are to read two short selections by the same author. They are to compare the two selections using a set of criteria brainstormed by the group. Possible criteria might be:

1. Fiction or non-fiction

2. Purpose—to inform or entertain?

3. Setting

4. Types of characters

5. Mood

The criterion used in the comparison will depend on the grade level of the students involved.

9. **Observation Reporting (Grades 5-8)**

   A. Purpose: To enhance critical thinking while teaching students to be alert observers.

   B. Materials: A selection of picture books.

   C. Introduction and Procedures: Each student is to select a short picture book to read to a primary class. The students are placed in groups of two. While the reader is sharing the book , the partner is taking notes on the behavior of the listeners. The partner writes a report on his/her observations. Based on the listeners' behavior, the observer must decide if the book was appropriate for a group of children. The students are to report their observations to the class.

10. **Listen for the Sentence that Does Not Fit (Grades 2-5)**

   A. Purpose: To develop the concept of story sense.

   B. Materials: A short picture book.

   C. Introduction and Procedures: The teacher should read one page of the picture book, adding a sentence that has nothing to do with the story. The students have to identify the sentence that doesn't belong. At the end of the activity, the teacher should read the book without interruption. For older students: Have students add a sentence to a different children's story and quiz their classmates.

11. **I'm Thinking of a Character (Grades 1-8)**

   A. Purpose: To develop language skills.

   B. Materials: A picture book or short story.

   C. Introduction and Procedures: The teacher should read aloud a story with multiple characters. The teacher begins the process by saying, "I'm thinking of a character in the story...I'm going to say one word. You are to guess the character." If a wrong guess is given, the teacher gives another describing word. The children continue to guess until someone identifies the correct character. The person who guesses correctly becomes the teacher and follows the teacher's example.

12. Scrambled Sentences (Grades 1-3)

A. Purpose: To promote oral language development and a sense of story.

B. Materials: Poster board cut into squares or sentence strips.

C. Introduction and Procedures: On each sentence strip or square, the teacher will copy either the beginning, middle, or ending parts of a story. Each student is given all three parts of one sentence and must sequence the sentence parts to make sense. The teacher then reads the picture book without interruption. Finally, the teacher rereads the story, hesitating so that each student can insert his or her sentence at the appropriate place in the story.

13. Holiday Story Categorization (Grades 1-5)

A. Purpose: To promote student understanding of the main idea using story book titles.

B. Materials: A selection of children's books or short stories pertaining to a variety of holidays.

C. Introduction and Procedures: The teacher writes a feature analysis containing holidays on the board or chart tablet as follows: (Additional holidays can be added or substituted).

Hanukkah	Christmas	Kwanzaa	Cinco de Mayo	Fourth of July

The teacher reads the name of each book and the group decides, by hearing the title only, which holiday is depicted in the story. As responses are given, the teacher writes the title under the suggested heading. Partners buddy read a story and report to the class as to whether or not the title was placed under the proper holiday heading. If the placement was incorrect, the expert partners (who read the story) make the change.

14. Where Does Your Story Take Place? (Grades 3-8)

A. Purpose: To develop student understanding of the importance of setting in narrative selections.

B. Materials: A world map, pins, yarn, string, or ribbon, and shelf paper.

C. Introduction and Procedures: Using an opaque (or Elmo) trace the outline of a world map on the shelf paper. Leave enough space around the border to provide space for illustrations. Fasten the paper to the wall or bulletin board. Each child should read a book and is encouraged to select a character or incident to illustrate. The students then use string colored yarn, or ribbon to connect their illustration with the country in which the story takes place.

15. Emotions (Grades K-2)

A. Purpose: To demonstrate how a reader's voice changes to fit the feelings of a character, as it does in speech.

B. Materials: A selection of children's books with themes that emphasize different emotions.

C. Introduction and Procedures: Before presenting the story to the class, the teacher should preread the story, practicing intonation which reflects the moods of the characters as they react to incidents in the story. The first reading of the story should be uninterrupted. During a subsequent reading the teacher should stop at peak times and ask how a character is feeling at that moment. Examples of books to select dealing with specific feelings are as follows:

Love   Munsch, Robert—*Love You Forever*
                 Gag, Wanda—*Millions of Cats*

Fear   Waber, Bernard—*Ira Sleeps Over*
                 Steig, William—*Sylvester and the Magic Pebble*

Loyalty   Daughtery, James—*Andy and the Lion*

Excitement   Sendak, Maurice—*Where the Wild Things Are*

16. Character Study (Grades 3-8)

A. Purpose: To promote critical thinking by comparing and contrasting characters in a story.

B. Materials: A selection of novels.

C. Introduction and Procedures: The students are to read a novel and choose two characters for a long term activity. A graphic similar to the following is completed by the students as they read their novels.

	Character's Name	Character's Nams
home		
personality		
appearance		
hobbies		
responsibilities		
age		

17. Compare and Contrast (Grades 3-8)

A. Purpose: To review story elements and provide practice in finding likenesses and differences.

B. Materials: A selection of children's books.

C. Introduction and Procedures: The following chart is displayed for the students.

Comparison	Title	Title	Title
author			
number of characters			
main theme			
setting			
plot			

This activity can be done independently, but is great for paired reading activities. Two students either read the same book or a book on a related theme. In their "buddy" groups, they discuss their books and complete the chart displayed across the front of the room. As more students complete their part of the front chart, more total group discussion related to likenesses and differences of story elements occurs. This activity also stimulates interest in reading a variety of novels.

18. Using Your Senses (Grades 2-8)

A. Purpose: To develop vocabulary through the classification and connection of known ideas with unfamiliar concepts.

B. Materials: A selection of children's books, chart paper and pencils.

C. Introduction and Procedures: This activity is teacher directed with primary children. The older students are instructed to read their book specifically looking for words that provide sensory impressions. Students work in heterogeneous groups of four to complete this task to enable students of all academic levels to participate. They divide the chart paper into four sections as follows:

Soft	Rough	Prickly	Hairy
silky	cement	whiskers	dog
downy	wood	cactus	paintbrush
foam	rasp	bur	rabbit
	tree bark		

Sensory words are placed in the appropriate columns as they are found. Debriefing as a class offers multiple opportunities for learning new words.

19. Is it Real? (Grades 1-4)

A. Purpose: To distinguish between real and make-believe.

B. Materials: A picture book, paper and pencils.

C. Introduction and Procedures: The children should number their papers down the left side of the page. The teacher then reads a sentence from a picture book. The children are to write "real" if it could happen, or "not real" if it is make-believe. Discuss the sentences in class.

20. Student Composed Questions (Grades 3-8)

A. Purpose: To develop students' thinking skills by providing opportunities for them to develop and answer each others' questions.

B. Materials: Paper & pencils and 4-6 copies of the same book for <u>each</u> group.

C. Introduction and Procedures: A group of 4-6 students each read the same book. Each student is directed to write six questions. One question should ask who, one what, one why, one where, and one how. These questions are given to students who are outside their group. The question writers form a panel and answer the questions that are posed to them by their classmates. This is an excellent activity to stimulate interest in different novels.

21. Following Directions (Grades 3-8)

A. Purpose: To give students practice in following directions.

B. Materials: A selection of "How to do it" books and a variety of art materials.

C. Introduction and Procedures: Put students in groups of four and give each group a craft book which contains demonstrations that are short and show finished products. Younger students may all do the same "how to" project with teacher direction.

22. Investigating Science Fiction (Grades 3-5)

A. Purpose: To provide practice in distinguishing between realism and fantasy.

B. Materials: A set of science fiction stories, paper, pencils.

C. Introduction and Procedures:

1. Discuss the characteristics of science fiction with students.

2. Read a short science fiction story to the class and have students identify which parts of it could be true and which could not.

3. Have students read another science fiction story and list the parts that could be true and those that could not.

4. Lead students to concluding that there is more that could possibly be true in older science fiction stories because of the advancement in space travel and technology. This is done by identifying the publication date of the books read.

23. Biography (Grades 3-8)

A. Purpose: To teach the term "biography" and to provide students with opportunities to experience a part of some important person's life.

B. Materials: A selection of biographies (varying reading levels), costume clothes, 3x5 cards, pencils.

C. Introduction and Procedures: The students select a biography. They are to read the biography with the specific purpose of getting a good picture of the person. They are to dress up like, and pretend to be that person while telling the class the story of his or her life. Each student is given a 3x5 card to record the name of his/her book, the author, when and where the person lived and why he/she is remembered. These cards can be displayed on a biography bulletin board.

24. Who, What, Where, When, How, Why? (Grades 3-8)

A. Purpose: To provide students with practice in reading with specific question words in mind.

B. Materials: A selection of children's books, paper, pencils.

C. Introduction and Procedures: The students are asked to divide the front and back of their paper into three sections each, as pictured in the example. The sections should be labeled, who, what, where, when, how, and why.

Front		
Who　Who	What　What	Where　Where
<u>Danny</u> looked out of the window.	<u>Snow</u> had covered the ground.	Carol ran <u>around the corner</u>.

Back		
When	How	Why
The <u>next</u> day we planned to leave.	Elizabeth ran <u>quickly</u> home.	Elizabeth ran <u>quickly</u> home <u>because she was scared</u>.

Students are to find sentences in their books that answer these question words and write them in the appropriate place on the chart, underlining the key answer word(s).

25. Literacy Circles Grades 3-8)

A. Purpose: To stimulate critical thinking and to provide experiences in working in a cooperative group.

B. Materials: Sets of books by the same author, paper, pencils.

C. Introduction and Procedures: Four or five students should read a different book by the same author. In addition, they should do an author search on the Internet. The group then discusses how the books are alike and different, noting if the kind book changed as the author grew older.

26. My Reading Record (Grades 3-8)

A. Purpose: To have student keep a record of the books they read.

B. Materials: A selection of children's books, paper and pencils, record form:

Date	Title of Book	Author	Fiction/ Non- fiction	Plot	Like

C. Introduction and Procedures: Each student is given a copy of the above form to keep track of the books he/she has read. At the end of a designated time, the students play the part of a news reporter and share this information with their classmates.

27. What's He Saying? (Grades 2-5)

A. Purpose: To use picture clues to enhance comprehension and to introduce the use of quotation marks.

B. Materials: A selection of picture books, drawing paper, crayons.

C. Introduction and Procedures: Each student should select a story to read. Next, they should choose a character to draw and include a caption next to him/her. Refer to the example shown below. Discuss quotation marks and their meaning.

28. Literature Bee (Grades 4-8)

A. Purpose: To gain a better understanding of various literature books, reviewing story elements.

B. Materials: Scoring materials, a list of questions, paper, pencils.

C. Introduction and Procedures: Before this game can be conducted successfully, several books should have been read and discussed by the class, with the main idea stressed. Then the children must become familiar with the rules of the literature bee.

Rules:

1. The teacher asks one team member a question and then switches to the first member of the other team.

2. If a team member answers the question correctly, that teams gets one point. An incorrect answer gets no point.

3. The team with the greatest number of points after every member on both teams has been asked a question is the winner. Once the preparation for the activity has been completed, the class should be divided into two teams with an equal number of members on each. The teacher proceeds to ask questions concerning the characters, plots, or particular incidents in the books. The teams stand in two lines and each member takes a turn answering a question.

29. Think Beyond the Text (Grades 3-8)

A. Purpose: To encourage higher order thinking and develop composition skills.

B. Materials: A variety of children's books or short stories.

C. Introduction and Procedures: Students assume the identity of the main character of a story they are reading. The students then write a letter to the class. In the letter they will share the experiences of the character and use their imagination to tell something new about "themselves" which was not specifically stated in the story. This activity is designed to stimulate interest in books or stories they have not yet read.

30. Dress-Up (Grades K-4)

A. Purpose: To promote oral language and stimulate creative thinking.

B. Materials: A collection of clothes for dress-up (Garage sales are the best for gathering a variety of different sizes and styles. Sometimes, children want to bring clothes to portray their character, as well.

C. Introduction and Procedures: A number of short stories or books should be read prior to attempting this activity. The children then decide on a character and select clothing for that character. The activity is structured like a Show-and-Tell exercise.

1. The class may ask only "yes" or "no" questions to determine what character is being portrayed.

2. After a set number of the questions, depending on the maturity of the students and the number of books read, the class is considered stumped and the character wins. A variation for this activity could have the dressed-up character tell something about the book and the students guess the name of the character.

31. The Book Television (Grades 3-8)

A. Purpose: To encourage reading and develop summarization skills.

B. Materials: Shelf paper, boxes, sticks, a selection of children's stories.

C. Introduction and Procedures: The students are divided into groups of four. Each group will have a different book. The four members of a group will be responsible for writing a summary of the book. From the summary, they are to decide on four drawings that best tell the story. These are drawn sequentially on the shelf paper. When the drawings are completed, the paper is rolled up in the form of a scroll with sticks at each end. Placed at each end of a box, this creates a television-type viewer. While one student gives the oral report, the others turn the sticks to unroll the story. See an illustration of the viewer below:

32. Illustrations Carry A Message (Grades K-5)

A. Purpose: To practice higher order thinking skills, and demonstrate how pictures affect the comprehension of a story.

B. Materials: The complexity of the book used in this activity should vary based on the age and maturity of the children. In any case, the selection should contain pictures with strong emotional content.

C. Introduction and Procedures: Choose a book that is unfamiliar to students. Show the children one picture and ask questions similar to the following:

   1. What do you think happened in this picture?

   2. Why is the child frightened?

   3. Who do you think will help him?

   4. Do you think his problems will be solved? How?

   5. What do you think caused his problem?

(Questions will vary with the picture) Complex wordless picture books are excellent sources to use with this activity. Examples include *Free Fall, Sector 7, or Tuesday,* by David Weisner.

33. Fact or Fiction (Grades 2-5)

A. Purpose: To develop critical thinking by distinguishing between fact and fiction.

B. Materials: Numerous short selections, both fiction and nonfiction, 3x5 cards, pencils.

C. Introduction and Procedures: Each student reads a short selection and completes a card similar to the follow:

Title:
Author:
Fact or Fiction:

They then trade selections with a partner and complete a card on their partner's selection. Finally, the partners have to decide what characteristics the selection had that made the be classified as fiction or nonfiction.

34. Cause and Effect (Grade 2-5)

A. Purpose: To develop critical thinking skills and help students understand cause and effect relationships.

B. Materials: Chart paper, markers, short story. C. Introduction and Procedures: Read a short story to the class. Divide the class into groups of four. Each group will be given a piece of chart paper and are to divide it into two columns as follows:

Cause	Effect
1.	
2.	
3.	

Give the students a list of causes and ask the groups to complete the "effect" side of the chart based on what happened after the incident occurred. After completing this, use another story to reverse the lesson listing the effects first, and the students giving the causes. Finally, older students can follow this process, analyzing a text for cause and effect relationships and completing both sides of the chart.

35. Making Inferences (Grades K-5)

A. Purpose: To teach students to make educated guesses based on a limited number of facts.

B. Materials: A picture book with large pictures, preferably, a "big book." C. Introduction and Procedures: Select a big book with a story containing a number of characters and very busy pictures.

With younger children this activity can be done as a total class. With older students, the activity works well in groups of four. In either case, begin by demonstrating the observational technique.

Example: Have students look at the first picture in the book *Little Black Goes to the Circus* by Walter Farley. Say "In this picture there are many things. You see Mr. Bruno with a top hat standing in front of a big tent. Beside him sits a monkey on a tricycle and a little boy sitting on Little Black, his pony. What can you tell me about this story just by looking at the picture?" Students keep this brainstormed list of responses to questions brought up by either the teacher or other group members. This is a pre-reading technique, so following this activity, students read the story to verify.

36. Scanning for Rhyming Words (Grades 2-5)

A. Purpose: To teach students to scan a selection to locate an answer.

B. Materials: A selection of books of poetry, enough for one per student, paper and pencil.

C. Introduction and Procedures: Give the students a specified number of minutes (3-5) depending on their age and maturity) to write down as many rhyming words as they can find in their book. This works well with partners. Each group reads their rhyming words. When the scanning for rhymes game is completed, the groups trade lists with each other. Their task is to write a two line poem using the rhyming words on the other groups list.

For example:

Original Poem: "Fire Fly" by Elizabeth Maddox Roberts

A little light is going by,
Is going up to see the sky,
A little light with wings.

I never could have thought of it,
To have a little bug all lit,

And made to go on wings.

Rhyming Words Chosen: by, sky, it, lit

Example two line poem: The stars in the sky,
                          Seemed to float on by.

37. Skimming Through the Alphabet (Grades 1-4)

A. Purpose: To teach students how to skim through text selections.

B. Materials: Pencils, Paper, Selection of picture books, enough for one per student.

C   Introduction and Procedures: Students are to letter their papers A to Z down the left side of their paper. When the teacher says "Go" students are to open their books and look for a word with an "a" in it, then a "b," and proceed through "z." They are to write these words next to the corresponding letter. The first person to write all the words through the letter "z" wins the game. The game can be made more difficult by requiring the letter to begin the word. The winner of the game can also be determined by setting a time limit.

38. Create a Creature (Grades K-4)

A. Purpose: To encourage students to think creatively and use their imagination.

B. Materials: A variety of pre-cut triangles, circles, squares, rectangles, octagons, or other shapes, pencils, crayons, paper, glue.

C. Introduction and Procedures: Read a fantasy story aloud. Maurice Sendak's, *Where the Wild Things Are*, is an excellent example of a children's story with funny creatures as characters. Children are to create a wild thing, beginning with one or more of the shapes provided. They will be using a mixture of art media to complete their wild thing.

Example:

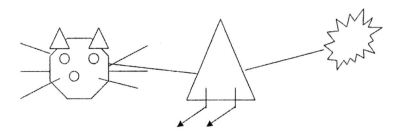

Using the language experience approach, get the students to dictate a story about their "wild thing." These stories can be shared in class.

39. Following Directions (Grades 2-4)

A. Purpose: To practice following directions using a creative interactive process.

B. Materials: A picture book, prepared sentence strips with directions, paper, pencils.

C. Introduction and Procedures: This activity is fun to do with a book that has already been shared with the students. The exercise starts with the teacher giving the title of the story. Example: *One Kitten for Kim* Then the teacher holds up a sentence strip that says, "Change each K to M." (*One Mitten for Mim*) Another sentence strip says, "Change the "i" in Mim to O. (*One Mitten for Mom*) Another sentence strip says, "Leave out the word that rhymes with kitten. *(One for Mom)* Another sentence strip says, "Write only the last word." (Mom) These activities are fun to do in groups. Older student like to create their own for other students to figure out.

40. Vacation Anyone? (Grades 3-5)

A. Purpose: To provide authentic reading and writing activities while improving reading comprehension and business letter writing.

B. Materials: A selection of short stories, picture books, paper, and pencils.

C. Introduction and Procedures: Each child should read a short story or picture book with settings somewhere in the area of study. Each student is to write a business letter to the Chamber of Commerce of the capital city of the state which is the setting of his/her book. The letter should request information on a particular location where they want to vacation. When the travel brochures come, the children should share them with the class. Students might also finish their letters and then send them as e-mail to the Chamber of Commerce of the selected location. Information and pictures could then be collected into a Power Point presentation by the student with assistance as necessary.

41. Name That Story (Grades 2-4)

A. Purpose: To develop the understanding of main ideas by providing titles for stories.

B. Materials: Selection of picture books, short stories, paper, pencils.

C. Introduction and Procedures: Read an unfamiliar short story to the class. Cover the title before reading the text and have students give the story a title immediately following reading. Have students write their choices on the board and ask students to vote on their favorite title. After their favorite has been identified, uncover the real title and compare it to the students' title. "Were we close? Do you like the author's title better than ours?" Repeat this process with another story. This activity works great with <u>short</u> stories as the intent is to focus on the "main" idea.

42. Intonation…Comprehension (Grades K-4)

A. Purpose: To emphasize the importance of punctuation marks in comprehension as we read or listen.

B. Materials: A picture book, three large cards with an exclamation mark, a question mark, or a period.

C. Introduction and Procedures: The teacher reviews: 1) question sentence using personal sentences like, "Do you like ice cream?" 2) Exclamation sentence using, "I <u>love</u> ice cream!" Then the teacher should read some sentences from a picture book to the class changing the intonation of his/her voice to show excitement or interrogation. Three students are given the punctuation cards. After each sentence is read, the class should decide which mark goes a the end of the sentence. When the activity is completed, the teacher should read the entire story to the students.

43. Who, What, When, Where, Why, How (Grades K-5)

A. Purpose: To enhance comprehension.

B. Materials: Sentence strips, butcher paper, markers, selected literature based on the age and reading level of the students.

C. Introduction and Procedures: A bulletin board should be prepared in advance, including as many of the question words as deem appropriate for the text and the level of the students involved.

Example:

Who?	What?	When?	Where?	Why?	How?
Goldi-locks	She broke the chair.	In the morning.	In the woods.	She was curious.	She sat on the chair.

1. The teacher should begin by writing some phrases from the text on sentence strips and distributing one to each student. The students must bring their strip to the front, place it under the appropriate question and tell why they placed it where they did.

2. Place the students in groups of four. Have them select another phrase from the same text and write it on a sentence strip. The rest of the class has to determine whether the phrase answers who, what, where, when, why, or how.

44. Live a Story (Grades K-3)

A. Purpose: To develop student understanding of fantasy in literature.

B. Materials: A fantasy story (*Where the Wild Things Are*, by Maurice Sendak for example), materials to make masks: paper plates, paper sacks, crayons, and markers.

C. Introduction and Procedures: The teacher reads the story aloud and after discussing the characters, the children are to select a character to portray. *Where the Wild Things Are,* works well because the entire class can be involved in acting out the story. Some could portray the wild things, some trees and plants, and one could be Max, one his mother and one his dog.

45. Echo Reading for Fluency (Grades K-5)

A. Purpose: To develop fluency and appropriate intonation, thereby promoting comprehension.

B. Materials: Selected children's literature written at the independent level for the students involved.

C. Introduction and Procedures: Divide the students into groups of four, heterogeneously. Two children read the first sentence of the story. The other children provide an echo by re-reading the same sentence. This can be modeled using the whole class prior to breaking into groups. It is important for upper elementary students to practice these intonation exercises. They are more readily willing to do this if they are preparing to do read alouds for the kindergarten classes in their school. This type of connection with kindergarten is also a positive experience for the five-year-olds, who see their older brothers and sisters learning to read, and noticing its importance.

Unit 6

Finding Information: Dictionary/Reference Skills

U sing reference materials is a vital study skill for success in academic literacy. The activities in Unit IV stress the importance of the dictionary, internet sources, book aids, and a variety of other reference materials. The lessons range in difficulty from simple alphabetizing to narrowing a topic when searching the internet.

Finding Information

Students have information which they would like to find, whether the information is for personal purposes or to be used for successful completion of schoolwork. The information might be on a particular subject, a list of books by a certain author, or a specific book or item of information. Libraries continue to be a center of focus for locating information. The older methods of research are still available; from the librarian, the card catalogs, the microfiche, large collections of documents in various forms, and a reference area with encyclopedias, dictionaries, almanacs, yearbooks, atlases, music, books on tape, videos, software programs, newspapers, periodicals, and other reference materials. Students still must learn to locate information, books, and other resources within the library and on-line.

Fiction, nonfiction, picture books, and biographies are usually grouped separately.

Dictionaries

Most of the dictionaries in school and public libraries are general dictionaries, each including words from general English for a general reader. There are also specialized dictionaries that define words used in a particular field or profession, art, or craft. Any one page in a general dictionary probably contains a few thousand words, but it probably defines only a few dozen. A word entry discusses the meanings and the various forms of the entry word or headword, which is the word in boldfaced type that begins the word entry. When you look up a word in a dictionary, you are looking for its word entry.

Let's analyze a sample word entry to see what kinds of information it offers.

> **Glad (glad) gladder, gladdest**. Adj. 1. feeling or expressing joy, pleasure, or satisfaction; happy. 2. causing joy or pleasure; pleasing: glad tidings. 3. very willing: Tom will be glad to go with you. [Old English glad bright, cheerful.]—gladly, adv.—gladness, n. Syn. Glad, happy, delighted mean expressing feelings of pleasure. Glad is generally used to convey a degree of pleasure ranging from pleased satisfaction to a feeling of elation: The sailors were glad to see land on the horizon. Happy suggests enjoyment brought about by the fulfillment of one's desires: The child was happy pounding away at his new drum. Delighted implies a quick and lively emotional reaction that is keenly felt and vividly expressed: Ben uttered a delighted hurrah when he saw our guest. Glad (glad) n. Informal. Gladiolus. [Latin gladiolus little sword, diminutive of gladius sword; referring to the plant's sword-shaped leaves.]

The Entry Word: The boldfaced word at the beginning of the entry is called the entry word. If this word can be divided at the end of a line, the divisions will be indicated by a raised dot. The word explicate, for example, is written ex pli cate. This means that you can divide the word after ex or after expli. In the sample word entry, glad cannot be divided; gladder and gladdest, however, can be divided. This entry word will also tell you when a compound word should be written as one word (as in lighthouse), when it should be written as two words (as in light meter).

Pronunciation: The correct way to say the word is shown immediately after the entry word and indicated in three ways: accent marks, phonetic symbols, and diacritical marks. In entry words with more than one syllable, accent marks indicate which syllable should be stressed. To check the meaning of the other marks and symbols, look at the pronunciation key that is usually located at the bottom of the page.

Inflected Forms: Plural forms of nouns, adjective forms, and forms of verbs in other tenses are included in an entry. In this case, we see that the comparative and superlative forms of glad are gladder and gladdest. When two spellings are connected with or, they are equally acceptable. However, when they are joined with also, the first spelling is preferred. For example, the dictionary show the plural of alga as "algae" also algas."

Parts of Speech: Abbreviations in italics indicates the part of speech of the entry word and other forms of the word. At the beginning of this entry, we see that glad is usually used as an adjective, but later we learn that the same spelling can be used as a noun.

Etymology: Many entries include the history of the word, or etymology. The entry for glad1 indicates that this word is based on an Old English word. The entry for glad 2 shows this word comes from Latin.

Most libraries or media centers now use computerized catalogs, have access to databases on CD-ROM or on-line, and have connections to the internet. Internet access can be from anywhere there is a computer connected to the internet. Using a computer at home is a big convenience. With computers, students can explore vast resources that were previously unavailable, quickly.

Using the Internet

The Internet is a computer-based, worldwide information network. As you research a topic, the Internet and World Wide Web allow students to identify, retrieve, and study documents without leaving their home, school, or library. They can also use electronic mail, or e-mail, to communicate with others interested in a specific topic or with experts on that topic. Library computers can probably link students directly to the Internet at no cost. If students are using a computer at home, a modem, a device that connects a computer to a telephone or cable line will be needed. Users must also subscribe to an Internet service provider. This service will connect a home computer to the Internet for a fee. Today's libraries offer personal computers for research on the Internet, as students move to the preferred use of on-line resources, especially in rural areas, where they are likely to be using search engines on the computer. Students can use computer searches to read newspapers and periodicals, and to search for information on topics of interest. Some databases allow students to search by topic, by type of publication, or by specific publication. Some databases allow students to review the table of contents of one issue of a magazine or to read any part of the articles that interest the student. Students can also select the years they want to search. For a subject search, a keyword, a word or a phrase is used to allow the computer to locate the desired information.

Understanding Addresses

The information on the Internet is organized by locations, or sites, each with its own address. A web address is also called a Uniform Resource Locator, or URL. Most addresses begin with http://, which stands for hypertext transfer protocol" and identifies a way in which information is exchanged among computers connected by the Internet. The last part of an address, or its suffix, indicates the type of site it is.

Here are some of the suffixes in use:

Suffix	Type of Site
.com	Commercial
.edu	Educational
.gov	Government
.mil	Military
.net	Network organization or Internet service provider
.org	Organization

Using Browsers

Each Internet service provider uses a specific browser, a program that locates and displays Web pages. Some browsers display only the text, or words, on a Web page; most will display both text and graphics (pictures, photos, and diagrams). Browsers also allow you to print or download part or all of a Web site. (Downloading means copying information from Internet files onto a computer hard drive or a diskette.) Browsers permit you to move from page to page within a site to a related one. Names of current browsers include Netscape Navigator and Internet Explorer.

Accessing Websites

Let's say students are now connected to the Internet. If they want to see the information offered at a certain site, they can enter the site's address on the computer screen and be transferred there. They can also access specific reference sources this way, such as the New York Times or Encyclopædia Britannica. Some of these sources are free, but to gain access to others, you must subscribe and pay a fee in addition to the cost of the online service. A screen will explain any extra charges that are involved and let students choose whether to continue.

Using Search Engines and Subject Directories

If students don't have a specific address in mind, they can search by keyword with the help of a search engine or a subject directory. Search engines are a type of software that uses a keyword to compile lists of related Websites. Internet service providers use certain search engines, but students can switch to a different one by entering its address. Many kinds of search engines are available, and they offer slightly different services. Some print the first sentence or two of the information offered at each Website, while other search engines list only the site's title and address. Some search engines offer to list additional Websites similar to those already on your screen. Subject directories are a kind of software that provides an excellent place to start a search if students haven't selected a specific topic yet. A subject directory first lists general topics. After they choose one, the directory offers a list of possible subtopics from which to select. The directory then offers several more lists of subtopics for students to consider, allowing them to further narrow your topic. Finally, it provides a page of links to Web sites that are related to the specific topic you have now chosen. For example, the search engine Yahoo! has a subjects directory that offers fourteen general topics to choose from, such as Arts and Humanities. Then Yahoo! lists subtopics for students to choose from, helping them to narrow their search and define their topic until they reach a page of related Websites.

Moving Around Websites

Often a word or phrase within the text of a Webpage or at the end of the file will provide a link to a related Website. These special words or phrases are called hyperlinks. They may be underlined or printed in a different color to make them easy to spot. When students click their mouse on a hyperlink, they'll immediately be transferred to another Website. To get back, they can click on the back arrow or a similar symbol at the top of the computer screen.

Using CD-ROM and DVDs

Technological advances create new research opportunities every day, so any discussion of the resources available quickly becomes out-of-date. Still, two resources are likely to be used for many years to come: CD-ROMs (Compact Disc-Read-Only Memory) and DVDs (Digital Video Discs). They can be used with a personal computer at home, at school, or at a library. Library computer catalogs are another example of electronic resources that are not part of the Internet. Some of the databases available at the library are actually on CD-ROMs purchased by the library; other databases accessible from library computers are part of the Internet.

Searching the Internet

To search on the internet, students need to use a general keyword, such as *animal*, which will get a long list of sources or matches or hits. Usually, only a few of the matches will be of use to the searcher. By using a more specific keyword, such as *dachshund*, the searcher can narrow down the list of matches to include only the useful ones. Searches can also include

Boolean search techniques, which offer different ways to combine words. A student can use these techniques to look for books in a computer catalog, to find articles in magazine databases, or locate information on the Internet.

Boolean techniques use the words *and, or, not,* and sometimes *near* or *adj.*	
and	If you combine two keywords with and (such as wetlands and conservation), the computer will list only sources that have both words. This kind of search results in far fewer matches, but many more of them relate to your topic. (Some programs use + in place of and: wetlands + conservation.
or	If you want information on either one of two related topics, link them with or, as in alligators or crocodiles. The computer will conduct two searches at once.
not	To eliminate a category of information from a search, use not. For example, if you want information about genetic disorders but not Down's Syndrome, you can enter genetic and disorders not Down.
near or adj.	Some computer programs allow searchers to use near or adj (adjacent) to locate sources, usually articles, that have two keywords used near each other. For example, you might use wildlife near preservation as your keywords. One program may list only those sources in which the keywords are within eight words of each other. Another program might allow the keywords to be fifteen words apart.

Enclosing a phrase in quotation marks (for instance, "preserving natural resources") tells the computer to find every book or article with exactly those words.

If students truncate, or shorten, the keyword by using an asterisk (*), the computer will search for all words that begin with the letters before the asterisk. For example, using experiment* as a keyword will tell the computer to list books or articles containing such words as experiment, experimental, experimented, experimenting, and experiments. By truncating your keyword, you make sure the computer doesn't overlook various forms of the word. Truncating can be used when the exact spelling of a word is not known.

Students can also use a "wildcard" by inserting a question mark(?) into certain words. For example, if you aren't sure whether to use woman or women, enter wom?n. Techniques of search have evolved to the point that as students become proficient with their searching, vast amounts of information are available on—line. Students need to be taught to find information in nonfiction books. The need to realize that these books have a title page, copyright page, table of contents, foreword, introduction, or preface. Other parts of a book that students could use as they search for information, include the index, the glossary, the bibliography, the appendix, and the afterword or epilogue.

Evaluating the Information That Was Found

Evaluation of resources is necessary. Students need to consider the author, the date of publication, the importance of the information in relation to the topic being researched, and investigate the author's reasoning. Not every book or article in the library or on its databases offers unbiased, valuable, reliable information. Students need to be taught to evaluate the author of each source of information and read any biographical information about him or her. Students need to consider whether the author is an expert in a certain field or simply someone who has opinions about it. Then students need to compare and contrast facts to determine whether all the sources are in agreement.

Finding Information Activities

1. Word Location (Grades 2-8)

A. Purpose: To help students locate words quickly and effectively in the dictionary.

B. Materials: A selection of books for students to use to obtain words to locate in the dictionary.

C. Introduction and Procedures: Students should first be given several words to use to practice locating words in a guided practice setting. These words could be collected from text being used in class or chosen from text that will soon be used in the classroom. The next step would be to have students collect words to use to practice finding words in the dictionary, either from favorite stories or books of interest. Students would need to be taught the alphabetical order of the dictionary and the purpose of the guide words that appear on each page.

2. Pronunciation Key (Grades 2-8)

A. Purpose: To enable students to tell how to pronounce unknown words.

B. Materials: A selection of picture books with some unknown words that can be used for practice with the pronunciation key in an age appropriate dictionary.

C. Introduction and Procedures: Begin by looking at picture books that are of high interest to the students in the class. Select words that appear in the books and use these words to teach students to use the pronunciation key. Students will have to be taught what the marks mean in the key, (bay (bâ). However it should be tied to need and interest. Some words are more important to students than others. Even adults find that they do not know the exact pronunciation of words that they can read but have never heard spoken. Students should be encouraged to self-collect words that they do not know how to pronounce, which can be used as the basis for future lessons and practice.

3. Multiple Definitions (Grades 2-8)

A. Purpose: To increase student awareness of multiple meanings for the same word.

B. Materials: A selection of picture books with words that have multiple meanings (bay, bow, dictionary appropriate to the student's age, pencils, and paper.

C. Introduction and Procedures: Select several words which have multiple meanings and guide students through the process of finding these words in the dictionary. Have students read the definitions and discuss the meanings, repeating the sentences as necessary.

Example: Sentence: The boy slid into second <u>base</u>.

Example: base—the lowest part of something; bottom.

base—a place where military forces are stationed.

<u>base</u>—any of four corners of a baseball infield that a player must touch to score a run.

Then have students practice the same activity with other words; later collecting words from their reading that also have multiple meanings.

4. Newspaper Scavenger Hunt (Grades 3-8)

A. Purpose: To have students explore the newspaper as a source of information.

B. Materials: Enough copies of the local newspaper for partners or groups of three. A list of questions that students are to answer by looking deeply into the newspaper.

C. Introduction and Procedures: Hand out the sheets of questions to each group and explain that they are to write out the answers using information from the newspaper. Distribute the newspapers and tell students to let the teacher know when they have found all of the answers.

Possible Questions:

1. Who has a sale on dresses this week?

2. What does the Pine Apple Shop sell?

3. Who sells garden hoses the cheapest this week?

5. Webquest (Grades 2-8)

A. Purpose: To have students locate some websites that contain exceptional pictures or items of information.

B. Materials: Computer with internet connection for each student or enough computers for students to take turns using the computer over an extended period of time during the school day.

C. Introduction and Procedures: Hand out the sheets listing the websites that students are to visit. Set up an activity to have students show that they have been to the website; either printing a page or answering a question that requires entry to the website.

Sample websites:

1. Sharing NASA:
   http://ic.arc.nasa.gov/ic/projects/learning/features/19 98/sharing_feat/sharing_feat.html
   http://www.nps.gov/interp/nasa/

2. NASA Space Image Libraries
   http://www.okstate.edu/aesp/image.html

6. **Locating Books Using the Dewey Decimal System (Grade 2-8)**

   A. Purpose: To develop students' skills in finding children's books in any library.

   B. Materials: Dewey Decimal system chart. C. Introduction and Procedures: Give students a list of books that are known to be in the library at the time of the activity. Have students use the Dewey Decimal System to locate the books on the list. A second part of the activity could include favorite books, fiction and non-fiction.

7. **Locating a Different Version of a Familiar Tale (Grade 2-8)**

   A. Purpose: To demonstrate to students the use of a search engine to locate different versions of the same tale.

   B. Materials: Computer with internet access.

   C. Introduction and Procedures: The teacher will show students see a copy of *Cinderella* from the school library, and ask students how they can see if there are other versions of the story. To locate a different version of the same story, they can use a search engine such as Google. By setting the address: http://www.google.com a student can type in "Cinderella" and watch what comes up. Or the student might type in a genre, such as "folktales" and see what comes up. More advanced searches can show that there are over four-hundred versions of Cinderella available today.

8. **Using the Dictionary (Grades 4-8)**

A. Purpose: To increase student ability to find the meaning of words in context.

B. Materials: Sentences from books or novels.

C. Introduction and Procedures: Show sentences taken from children's novels which include unfamiliar words. Discuss the context. Ask: What do we think the word means? Ask for predictions. Write the predictions on the board.

    Example: Everyone was so tall around me. I felt like I was <u>sandwiched</u> between them.

           What does sandwiched mean? Does it mean something to eat?

           Look it up in the dictionary. Discuss the dictionary definition.

Ask students to scan a novel, finding an unfamiliar word. They must then copy the sentence, write their predictions as to the word's meaning and the dictionary definition.

9. **Using the Index (Grades 3-8)**

A. Purpose: To develop student ability to use the index to locate information in text.

B. Materials: A selection of non-fiction children's books.

C. Introduction and Procedures: Discuss the index as an alphabetical listing of important topics, people, and subtopics that generally are placed at the end of the book. The index reflects the page number where the information can be found. Discuss the concept of cross-referencing. (Disney, Walt, 45...See also Donald Duck)

In groups of four, students create an index for children's books with five questions for another group to answer. The groups meet together at the end of the activity to check each other's answers.

10. Puns Are Fun (Grades 2-5)

A. Purpose: To connect multiple meanings with children's literature.

B. Materials: A selection of children's books with multiple meanings in the text; examples include: *Cinderella Bigfoot* and *Hansel and Pretzel* by Mike Thaler.

C. Introduction and Procedures: Students will be introduced to multiple meaning words and then asked to listen for similar such words in the stories. Later, students will be asked to include multiple meaning words in their own writings.

Fairy godmother . . . . dairy godmother.

The princess and the pea . . . . the princess and the piano.

Cinderella wanted
    her toe to fit . . . . Cinderella Bigfoot needed a tow truck.

11. Alphabetical Order (Grades 3-5)

A. Purpose: To teach alphabetical order.

B. Materials: A selection of picture books, one per child.

C. Introduction and Procedures: The teacher divides the class into four groups. Every student gets a book. Each group must line its books up against the wall in alphabetical order. When the books are all lined up against, the groups will change places, serving as a check of their classmates' work.

12. ABC Foods (Grades 2-4)

A. Purpose: To develop vocabulary and teach alphabetical order.

B. Materials: A selection of nonfiction books dealing with kinds of food, paper, and pencils.

C. Introduction and Procedures: The teacher divides the class into five groups. The children are to look in their books for the names of foods and write one for each letter of the alphabet:

> Example: A   Apple
>
>   B   Bread
>
>   C   Carrots
>
>   D   Dessert

This activity could be made more complex by sorting the food by food group, as the ABC book is completed.

13. Guide Words (Grades 3-5)

A. Purpose: To teach dictionary skills.

B. Materials: A selection of picture books, paper, and pencils.

C. Introduction and Procedures: Each child is given a picture book and is instructed to find five words beginning with b, c, or d and write them on his/her paper. The teacher discusses dictionary guide words and explains that we are going to place the words on a pretend dictionary page. The teacher should make the sample dictionary pages on the chalkboard like the example shown below. Each student should read and spell the words one at a time and have the class decide on which page to put each word.

Bad bell	bet bun	cat cent	cell cup	dad den	dim dry

14. Connecting Guide Words to Personal Reading (Grades 3-8)

A. Purpose: To develop dictionary skills in a motivating way.

B. Materials: A dictionary for each student; a selection of children's books.

C. Introduction and Procedures: The teacher reviews the definition of a guide word and writes two guide words from a page in the dictionary. (The guide word on the left is the first entry and the guide word on the right is the last entry on the page.) Students work in groups of four to create a dictionary page. The words on their dictionary page should come from their novel.

15. Look It Up (Grades 3-5)

A. Purpose: To locate information in encyclopedias and other reference books.

B. Materials: Picture books, encyclopedias, and nonfiction books relating to a particular geographic area.

C. Introduction and Procedures: Read a picture book or short story to the class. Talk about where the story takes place. Choose a book which has a setting in a different geographic area than your location. Divide the class into six groups. Give each a topic to study which deals with the location under study. The topics could be as follows:

   1. The weather in the area.

   2. Places to visit.

   3. The kind of land in the area.

4. Industry or factories.

5. The population and kinds of people.

6. History of the area.

During a debriefing session, the groups would report their findings.

16. Using the Index (Grades 3-5)

A. Purpose: To teach children to use an index to get information.

B. Materials: Provide paper, pencils, and a selection of nonfiction book dealing with a large variety of things that fall into one class, such as animals. For example, a book about animals would contain an index with the names of all different animals and where to locate information in the book.

C. Introduction and Procedures: Each student is given a book like the one described. All of the books should be about the same topic, such as animals. Give the students a list of questions to answer. The questions should deal with the page on which you would find the information on specific animals.

Sample Questions:

1. Where can you find Siberian tigers?

2. What page has a picture of a male lion?

3. Where can we find out about cheetahs?

4. What page has a picture of the habitat of a leopard?

17. Using the Table of Contents (Grades 2-5)

A. Purpose: To gain information from the table of contents.

B. Materials: A selection of library books with tables of contents in them, paper, and pencils.

C. Introduction and Procedures: Each child chooses a partner and is given a book. His/her job is to prepare a set of questions for his/her partner to answer. The teacher should write a sample set of questions on the chalkboard as well as a make-believe table of contents. Example:

Table of Contents	*Questions*
Tracey's Cat 17	On what pages would you find a mystery?
I Wonder Why? 19	On what pages would you find something about animals?
The Mystery 25	In what pages would you find something about a little boy?
What Happened? 35	On what pages would you find somebody asking questions?

18. Using a Thesauruses (Grades 2-8)

A. Purpose: To encourage students to expand their vocabularies using a thesaurus.

B. Materials: A collection of age appropriate books, a thesaurus for each student, paper, and pencils.

C. Introduction and Procedures: Students need to be taught that a thesaurus provides synonyms for words. Using words self-collected from books that students are reading, students should be guided through finding synonyms for these words in the thesaurus. Later students need to collect words from their own writing and be asked to substitute the synonyms they find and engage in the re-writing process. Students can then be asked to read their old sentence and their new sentence to increase the vocabulary of the class.

19. Using the Card Catalog (Grades 3-5)

A. Purpose: To learn to use the card catalog.

B. Materials: Provide index cards, pencils, a file box, and a selection of books.

C. Introduction and Procedures: The teacher writes a sample card from the card catalog on the chalkboard.

Example:

```
        F
        Bur     Burch, Robert
        Renfro's Christmas, New York, Viking, 1968.

   59 p. illus.
```

The teacher should discuss the meaning of the "F" and the abbreviations for page (p.) and illustrated (illus.). Each child should be given a book and should be instructed to make a card to go in our room card catalog. When each child finishes, he/she puts his/her card in the file box, making sure the cards are alphabetical order. The alphabetical order is checked by each student as he places his card in the card catalog.

20. Evaluating Websites (Grades 3-8)

A. Purpose: To assist students in evaluating websites, understanding sources of information.

B. Materials: Books that students are reading, computer with access to the internet.

C. Introduction and Procedures: Students will be asked to research topics of their choice within a range of topics. Traditional sources as well as internet sources will be used to gather information. Students will then be guided through a process of information gathering while at the same time, listing the information that can be collected about each of the websites used during information collection for the research projects. Students will then be asked to consider the importance of sources of information and judge if there are some that need to be rejected among those found on the internet. Examples: Student websites posted by other schools, unverified, or unidentified websites where the source is unknown.

Unit 7

Composition/Writing Mechanics

W riting and reading are generally considered reciprocal processes, and because of this, are mutually supportive. Through read-alouds, children discover pictures and words in stories that are read to them. They begin to draw and scribble, and over time realize that these scribbles have meaning. Some children enter kindergarten with this awareness, while others lack the home literacy experiences to promote such learning. Teachers have to structure a language-rich classroom environment to facilitate this learning. To develop a community of learners, the teacher provides opportunities for students to read and write in authentic real-life activities. Students need to be allowed to self-select topics for composition.

Writing instruction also "involves learning to express meaningful ideas and use conventional spelling, grammar, and punctuation to express those ideas" (Tomkins, 2003, p.15). "Grammar and punctuation are best taught in meaningful contexts, in which language is used for real purposes" (Cox, 2002, p.430). "Students can play with words and sentences, through classification, forming patterns, and combining sentences. Children's literature is an excellent model for language use; student should be encouraged to play with the forms and structures of stories. It is during the revising and editing stages of writing that students apply their underlying knowledge of grammar, punctuation, and handwriting. Children learn to use language by using it" (Cox, 2002, p.430). However, the main purpose of all language is to communicate meaning.

Integrating reading and writing enhances reading comprehension. Unit VII focuses on the interrelationship of the two by providing direct experiences with different types of literature. The activities will require students to analyze the organization of texts to determine what makes them a narrative or what makes them an expository text. This will facilitate the development of composition in students. Responding to the different types of literature is the focus of Unit VII. In one example, one activity requires students to read a high action story and then rewrite the story in the form of a play. Students work in groups and are instructed to:

1. Divide the actions into three acts.

2. Decrease the number of characters to three.

3. Develop the characters through conversation.

4. Create backdrops.

5. Write stage directions wherever needed (door slamming, etc.)

6. Present their play to the rest of the class. This activity directly addresses the narrative genre and makes students aware of the major components of a play (character, time, setting, sound effects, stage directions, cues, etc.).

Composition/Writing Mechanics
Activities

1. **Autobiography (Grades 3-8) Informative**

    A. Purpose: To provide experiences with creative writing.

    B. Materials: A selection of autobiographies of varying readability levels, paper and pencils.

    C. Introduction and Procedures: To introduce the idea of autobiography, students will develop a timeline depicting the major events in their lives. Then, as they read their selected autobiography, they will complete a timeline on the famous person. Upon completion of the timeline, students will select one event to develop into a composition.

2. Fractured Fairy Tales (Grades 3-8) Narrative

A. Purpose: To develop higher order thinking skills and composition skills.

B. Materials: A selection of books containing fairy tales, paper and pencils.

C. Introduction and Procedures: Each group of four students reads a familiar fairy tale and makes a list of the characters in the story. Two groups meet together and give one of their characters to the other group to include in their story (Put one of the seven dwarfs in Cinderella). They rewrite the fairy tale changing it to include the new character.

3. Rewrite the Titles (Grades 3-8) Informative

A. Purpose: To develop composition skill and use of the thesauri.
B. Materials: Thesaurus, selection of children's literature.

C. Introduction and Procedures: The teacher writes the titles of a selection of children's books on the board, underlining key terms. In groups of four, students are to look up the underlined words in the thesaurus and reword the titles of the books.

For example:

The <u>Teacher</u> from
    the <u>Black</u> <u>Lagoon</u>   The Instructor from the Neon Bayou

Little <u>*Women*</u>   Tiny Ladies

4. Pretend to be an Animal: Keep a Diary (Grades 3-8) Narrative

A. Purpose: To develop higher order thinking skills and composition.

B. Materials: A selection of non-fiction books about animals, paper and pencils.

C. Introduction and Procedures: The students are instructed to read about a particular animal, paying close attention to the animal's habitat, enemies, and the food it eats. Students are to write a diary entry, or a day in the life of their animal.

5. Join the Story (Grades 3-8) Narrative

A. Purpose: To develop narrative writing in the first person.

B. Materials: A selection of novels with varying reading levels, paper and pencils.

C. Introduction and Procedures: Following the reading of a novel, students are to choose their favorite event and rewrite that event adding themselves as a character and writing in the first person. This process should be demonstrated as a class before having students attempt to do it independently. A short story can be used effectively in a group situation.

6. Grocery Lists (Grades 2-5) Informative

A. Purpose: To develop creative thinking skills.

B. Materials: A selection of picture books, grocery as from local papers, paper and pencils.

C. Introduction and Procedures: This activity can be done individually, in groups of four, or with the total class. After the books is read, students are to think about the characters in the story they read, and pretend they are going to the store to buy groceries for one week. They are to create a grocery list.

An excellent interdisciplinary extension would have them plan balanced meals using foods from their grocery list.

7. **Limericks/Poetry (All grade levels, teacher directed withy primary students)**

    A. Purpose: To develop creative thinking and encourage language development.

    B. Materials: A selection of short stories or children's books.

    C. Introduction and Procedures: Read aloud several examples of limericks, emphasizing the structure of the poem.

    Write an example on the board, with the structure:

    There was a dog named . . . .

    Line 1 _____ a
                                    rhyme
    Line 2 _____ a

    Line 3 _____ b
                                    rhyme
    Line 4 _____ b

    Line 5 _____ a

    Although limericks are supposed to be silly and be just for fun, they can be used to assist students in retaining difficult content information. Students are to write a limerick about the main character of their children's book. This is fun in groups of four.

8. **Cinquain Poems/ Poetry (All grades, teacher directed at primary level)**

    A. Purpose: To develop creative thinking and composition.

    B. Materials: A selection of children's books.

C. Introduction and Procedures: Explain the structure of a cinquain poem, doing some examples with the students. Write the structure on the board.

title	snow
describe the title	cold, white
action action action	falling, chilling, stopping
feeling about the title	people stay at home
title	snow

Students are to write a cinquain about a story element in the children's book read. (This can be about the character.)

9. **Diamante Poems/Poetry (All grade levels, teacher directed at primary level)**

A. Purpose: To develop creative thinking skills and composition.

B. Materials: A selection of children's books.

C. Introduction and Procedures: Explain the structure of the diamante poem, doing some examples on the board.

noun	night
two adjectives	dark, black
three participles	Sleeping, dreaming, relaxing
four nouns or a phrase	nobody is moving
three participles noting change	yawning, stretching, standing
two adjectives	bright, sunny
contrary noun	daylight

10. **Make the Plural Form (Grades 2-4)**

A. Purpose: To provide students with practice in making plurals.

B. Materials: Provide a selection of picture books, paper and pencils.

C. Introduction and Procedures: Each child is given a picture book and is instructed to write down fifteen words from the book which name things. Then they should choose a partner and trade words with him or her. The children are to make the plural form of all of their partner's words. After completing this, the children should take turns reading and spelling the plural to the class.

11. Reading/Writing Connections (Grades 2-8)

A. Purpose: To increase student awareness about the connection between Reading and Writing.

B. Materials: A collection of children's literature, previewed for quality.

C. Introduction and Procedures: Students will have a children's book read to them. They will be told prior to reading the book that they will be asked to write a response to the book. The book needs to evoke emotion, include a good story, and set the scene for writing. Students will then listen to the story and then teacher and students will write for 15-20 minutes. Responses may be shared.

12. Illustration as Pre-Writing (Grades 1-5)

A. Purpose: To provide a pre-writing activity for students.

B. Materials: A collection of picture books.

C. Introduction and Procedures: Students will listen to a several picture book read by the teacher. Students will then be asked to draw a picture illustrating one scene from the stories. Students will the use the picture to write a story based on the picture they drew. The story can be shared or be used in the writing processes of revision, editing, and publishing.

13. Scavenger Hunt Revision (Grades 2-8)

A. Purpose: To assist students in improving their writing by including language conventions and literary devices correctly in their own writing.

B. Materials: Students will need to create a piece of their own writing for use in this activity, perhaps during a Reading/Writing Connection, paper, and pencils.

C. Introduction and Procedures: Students will take a piece of their own work and after having a mini-lesson on a language convention or literary device, they will revise their piece of writing to include the convention or literary device in their writing. Students are guided through the process of revision with purpose.

Student Sentence:	I was skating at the rink on Saturday.
Language Convention:	gerand phrase
New Student Sentence:	Roller skating is my favorite thing to do on Saturday.

This activity could be extended to include giving students or groups of students points for correctly including a specified language convention or literary device correctly into a piece of their own writing.

14. History Comes Alive (Grades 2-8)

A. Purpose: To create authentic writing tasks for students.

B. Materials: Textbooks and children's books on the topic being discussed in class, paper and pencils.

C. Introduction and Procedures: After receiving mini-lessons on friendly letters, students are to write letters as if they are historical characters, storybook characters, or political figures; whatever fits the topic of the day. Students would use the children's books to gain a better picture of what the character would write about. Revision could take place as more is known about the characters.

Examples: George Washington writing a letter to Martha; George Bush to his mother Barbara; other letters that might have been written.

15. Author Exploration (Grades 2-5)

A. Purpose: To increase student skills in reporting information.

B. Materials: Children's literature written about one author, multiple books several authors.

C. Introduction and Procedures: In groups, students will read all of the materials provided about their author and then brainstorm as many things as possible that they have found to be true about the author. Then each group will write summaries of the information collaboratively and present their author to the class.

16. Add My Literary Device (Grades 2-8)

A. Purpose: To promote student familiarity with literary devices and their uses.

B. Materials: Nonfiction textbooks and children's books.

C. Introduction and Procedures: After students receive mini-lessons on literary devices, students will be given sentences and passages from nonfiction texts to use during this activity. Students, either individually or in groups will correctly insert a literary device. Students will be guided through the process with assistance as necessary. The new sentences are then read to lead into discussions of correct use and meaning.

17. History Comes Alive/ Descriptive (Grade 2-8)

A. Purpose: To increase student descriptive writing skills.

B. Materials: History textbooks, pencils, and paper.

C. Introduction and Procedures: Have students choose a person from history and find as many pictures of the person as possible. Then, using the pictures, students are to write a description of the person. Students will then be read the descriptions of the historical persons and choose which picture and person the description is referring.

Students will then brainstorm anything else that could be used to improve the description and revise their description. The new descriptions will be read to another class and the students will pick the person described.

18. Peanut Butter Sandwich (2-8)

A. Purpose: To add practical purpose to the process of revision of student composition.

B. Materials: Bread, peanut butter, table knife.

C. Introduction and Procedures: Students are asked to brainstorm the steps or directions to making a peanut butter sandwich. After all the ideas are collected and written down by a student, a student will then be asked to read the summary while another student carries out the described steps. Depending on the success of the student in making the sandwich, revision of the summary would be processed until a successful set of directions have been developed.

19. Bedrock Description (Grades 2-5)

A. Purpose: To increase students' skills in the area of descriptive writing.

B. Materials: Rocks of various types, sizes, and shapes, paper, and pencils.

C. Introduction and Procedures: Students will listen to the story, *Everybody Needs a Rock*, by Byrd Baylor, and then choose a rock from a collection provided. After looking closely at the rock the student will name the rock based on the attributes of the rock. Students will then be challenged to write a description of the rock that will enable other students to find their rock in a pile of rock on a student desk using the written descriptions provided by the students. Revision could be discussed by student as to how to enable students to distinguish any rocks that were not described well enough to be picked out easily.

20. Principal Persuasion (Grades 3-8)

A. Purpose: To demonstrate an authentic purpose for composition using persuasion.

B. Materials: Pencils and paper.

C. Introduction and Procedures: Students will be given a list of possible topics to be used as the content of their persuasive compositions. Students may want to add to the list. Students will then write a composition, addressed to the campus principal, that seeks to persuade the principal to do something on the list of topics or on a topic approved by the teacher. Students will then share their compositions in groups, discussing what might be added to increase the likelihood of the principal accepting their position.

Examples: Offering special items to the lunch menu; allowing students to have a special speaker at an assembly; allowing favorite music to be played over the PA system during lunch, etc.

21. Mystery (Grades 3-8)

A. Purpose: To give students opportunities to develop their creative writing.

B. Materials: Mystery books, paper, and pencils.

C. Introduction and Procedures: Each student is instructed to read a mystery book and write a summary of the main plot. The summary should include all of the main characters and the part they play in unraveling the mystery at hand. The students trade summaries and write the ending to their partner's book. After this is done, the partners discuss the true ending of their stories.

22. Characterization (Grades 3-8)

A. Purpose: To provide practice for students in creative writing.

B. Materials: A selection of novels, paper, and pencils.

C. Introduction and Procedures: The students are instructed to read a novel thinking about the personality of a main character. They are to make a list of adjectives they feel describe the main character. Then, they are to write a new adventure for the main character, pretending that three years have passed. They are to plan events in their story which depict the same characteristics of the main character in their original book.

23. Tongue Twisters (Grades 3-8)

A. Purpose: To develop students' ability to use alliteration and assonance in writing.

B. Materials: A book of tongue twisters, pencils, and paper.

C. Introduction and Procedures: The teacher reads some tongue twisters to the students and the students try to repeat them. The students are to make up their own tongue twisters to share with the class. Lower level students could be given a list of words which all begin with the same letters to give them a start.

1. Sally sells seashells by the seashore.

2. Fuzzy Wuzzy was a bear.
    Fuzzy Wuzzy had no hair.
    Fuzzy Wuzzy wasn't fuzzy,
    Was he?

3. New linoleum

4. Toy boat

5. Peter Piper picked a peck of pickled peppers.

24. Folk Tales (Grades 3-8)

A. Purpose: To provide practice in creative writing.

B. Materials: A selection of folk tales, paper, and pencils.

C. Introduction and Procedures: The teacher selects a couple of folk tales to read to the students. After discussing the idea of folk tales, the teacher reads the beginning of a folk tale to the students. The characters should be introduced and the main idea started when the teacher stops reading. The students are to work in groups of four to write a continuation of the folk tale. The first member of each group will write for about ten minutes before passing the story to the second member of the group. All four students in the group will add to the story. The new creations should be shared with the class.

25. Add a Character (Grades 3-8)

A. Purpose: To provide practice in creative writing using the first person.

B. Materials: A selection of novels with varying reading levels, paper, and pencils.

C. Introduction and Procedures: The students are to read a novel and choose their favorite event in the book. They are to rewrite the event adding themselves as a character and write in the first person. It would be helpful to do this as a class before having students do it independently. A short story could be used to do this as an introduction to this activity.

26. Write a Letter (Grades 3-8)

A. Purpose: To provide practice in writing to persuade and while practicing a different method of book reporting.

B. Materials: A selection of books, paper, and pencils.
C. Introduction and Procedures: Each student is to read a book of his/her choice. The teacher is to review the format of a friendly

letter with the class. Each student is to write a letter to a friend trying to encourage the friend to read this book. The letter should include a description of the main characters and information on the major plot.

27. Book Report Form (Grades 3-8)

A. Purpose: To provide practice writing couplets as well as stimulate independent reading.

B. Materials: A selection of books, paper, and pencils. C. Introduction and Procedures: Each student is to read a book and then write a poem about it. Prior to the writing, the class will brainstorm possible words to use in couplets, using ideas from the books selected.

An example follows:

> I read a book name The Enchanted Fawn,
> I stayed awake reading 'til dawn.
> From the enchanted water he did drink,
> And a fawn he became, as quick as a win.

28. Interview the Author (Grades 3-8)

A. Purpose: To encourage students' critical thinking and give practice in writing.

B. Materials: A selection of novels, paper, and pencils.

C. Introduction and Procedures: Each student is to read a novel and then write a pretend interview with the author. The interview can be between the student and the author, or between a character in the book and the author. The teacher might supply the students with some suggested questions to stimulate their thinking.

For example:

1. Where did you get your ideas for writing this book?

2. Did you really live in the …?

3. Did you have a family?

If the student is writing the interview between the author and a character, the character might ask questions like:

1. Why did this have to happen?

A variation of this activity has two students read the same novel to facilitate the brainstorming of interview questions. These questions could be used in a role play situation.

29. Hobbies (Grades 3-8)

A. Purpose: To encourage higher order thinking and develop students' composition skills.

B. Materials: A selection of books on hobbies, paper, and pencils.

C. Introduction and Procedures: The teacher will brainstorm, with students, different hobbies they or people they know have, making a list on the board. Students are then shown a variety of books on different hobbies. Students are to select a hobby that might be of interest to them. They use the book as a reference to write a short informational composition on the hobby. In their composition, they should tell what sparked their interest in that hobby.

30. Circus Life (Grades 3-8)

A. Purpose: To stimulate students' independent reading and creative writing.

B. Materials: A selection of circus stories, paper, and pencils.

C. Introduction and Procedures: Each student is to read a circus story. These stories do not have to be long and the same story can be read by a number of students. The teacher discusses with the class, the many circus related occupations. Each student is to pretend he/she is a circus person and write about the circus performance from his/her person's point of view. The many occupations include the different performers, the ringmaster, animal trainers, ticket takers, cooks, and concession stand workers.

31. Let's Pretend (Grades 3-8)

A. Purpose: To stimulate student's higher order thinking skills and develop composition skills.

B. Materials: A selection of books relating to the zoo, paper, and pencils.

C. Introduction and Procedures: Each student is to read a book about the zoo. This book can be fiction or nonfiction. The students are instructed to pretend they are an animal at the zoo. They are to write about one day at the zoo, telling what they are thinking when people come up to look at them and what the people seem to be thinking.

32. Writing to Persuade (Grades 3-8)

A. Purpose: To increase students' skills in writing to persuade.

B. Materials: A selection of fiction books, paper, and pencils.

C. Introduction and Procedures: During this activity, students are to create an advertisement to sell a book they have read, and then write a letter to a friend to persuade the friend to read it. The advertisement must include the main idea of the story, include something exciting about one of the characters, (not give the ending of the story) and tell why they think others will like the book.

33. Just So Stories (Grades 2-8)

A. Purpose: To increase students' skills in writing to persuade.

B. Materials: Some "Just So Stories," paper, and pencils. C. Introduction and Procedures: The teacher should familiarize the students with "Just So Stories" by reading some of Kipling's. "How the Lion Got His Roar" is a good example. The students are to write a "Just So Story" about an animal. The story can be about a real animal or a funny one about a make-believe animal made up of parts of several animals. An example would be, "How the Snake Grew Legs on Which to Walk." This activity can be done with primary students as a teacher-directed activity.

34. Create a Data Chart (K-3)

A. Purpose: To introduce informational writing.

B. Materials: Big Book about a specific animal.

C. Introduction and Procedures: The teacher will share the big book with the students, emphasizing the animals environment, its enemies, its body characteristics, and the food it eats to survive. Then the teacher draws the data chart on the board.

Example:

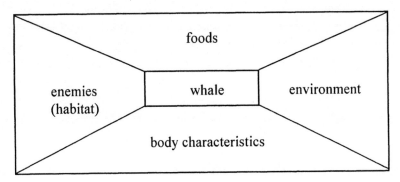

Ask students questions about the animal and as their responses are received, place them in the appropriate section of the data chart. This can be done in pictures, words, or phrases. After the chart is completed, students are to write informative sentences, or paragraphs using the information in the data chart. Complexity will depend on the age and ability of the students involved.

35. Write an Autobiography (Grades 3-8)

A. Purpose: To provide students with experiences in creative writing while learning the meaning of the word "autobiography."

B. Materials: A selection of autobiographies, paper, and pencils.

C. Introduction and Procedures: The student is to read an autobiography in order to write about a person's life or a recent event in that person's life. However, to make this activity meaningful, students will write a portion of their own autobiography selecting either an early or recent event in their life to discuss. The response from the autobiography will be written after students discuss their personal reflections in class.

36. Write a Movie Script (Grades 3-8)

A. Purpose: To provide students with experiences in creative writing.

B. Materials: A selection of good action stories, paper, and pencils.

C. Introduction and Procedures: The teacher should read an action story to the class. This can be a short story. The class develops a movie script from events in the short story. This is written on the board to serve as a model. The students are instructed to read a story and develop a move script about the story. This can encompass the whole story or simply dwell on one incident in the story. This activity is great for cooperative groups.

37. Fairy Tales (Grades 3-8)

A. Purpose: To provide students with experience in creative writing.

B. Materials: A selection of book containing fairy tales, paper, and pencils.

C. Introduction and Procedures: The students are to select a fairy tale to read. They are to rewrite the fairy tale making the hero the villain and the villain the hero. These rewritten fairy tales should be shared with the class.

38. Write a Story (Grades 3-8)

A. Purpose: To provide students with experiences in creative writing.

B. Materials: A selection of short novels at varying reading levels, paper, and pencils.

C. Introduction and Procedures: Each student selects a book to read. The teacher appoints partners. Each student is to read his/her story and then provide his/her partner with the following information.

    1. Name of the book.

    2. Main characters, with a description of each one.

    3. Setting and time of the story.

    4. The problem or action based on the plot.

    5. A list of 15 vocabulary words from the story. These words should be ones the reader doesn't know or at least doesn't see often.

The partner is to rewrite the story based on the above information and using as many of the vocabulary words as he/she can.

39. Write a Telegram (Grades 3-8)

A. Purpose: To provide students with practice in summarizing and being concise.

B. Materials: A selection of books, paper, and pencils. C. Introduction and Procedures: Each student is to read a story and write a telegram about the story, using 20 words or less. The telegram is delivered to his/her partner. The partner is to write a report of the book, using only the 20-word telegram and the story title. These reports should be at least 50 words. When the reports are finished, the partners share the original stories and the new ones.

40. Sell Your Book (Grades 3-8)

A. Purpose: To provide students with practice writing to persuade.

B. Materials: A selection of novels, paper, and pencils.

C. Introduction and Procedures: The students are instructed to read a book and then write an advertisement for it. The advertisement should be displayed on the bulletin board. The students should include information on where the book can be found and why it is do great!

41. Write a Title (Grades 3-8)

A. Purpose: To provide students with practice in summarizing to write a story title.

B. Materials: A collection of children's magazines, articles, or newspapers that can be cut, poster board, and scissors.

C. Introduction and Procedures: The students are instructed to cut out some short articles and paste them on the poster board. The students are to cut off the story title and exchange stories with someone. Each student is to write a title for the stories given to him/her by his/her partner. The partners then share the original title.

42. Job Descriptions (Grades 3-8)

A. Purpose: To provide students with practice in creative writing while learning about possible occupations.

B. Materials: A selection of fiction or nonfiction books dealing with a variety of occupations, paper, and pencils.

C. Introduction and Procedures: Students are instructed to read a book about a particular job in which they are interested. They are to write a job description to share with the rest of the class. Their job description should give the following information:

1. Type of job.

2. Location or setting of the job.

3. Hours to be worked.

4. Education required.

5. Experience required.

6. Vacation allowed.

7. Other fringe benefits.

43. Story Titles (Grades 3-8)

A. Purpose: To provide students with practice in creative writing as well as in developing imagination.

B. Materials: A selection of books or a list of book titles, pencils, and paper.

C. Introduction and Procedures: The students are instructed to use the story titles to construct a sensible story. This is more fun when done in groups. For example, a story might be as follows:

The Boy Next Door was really an *All American*. He wants a *Rookie First Baseman* and great at everything he tried. He want to go on an *Incredible Journey*.

44. Be an Exchange Student (Grades 3-8)

A. Purpose: To provide practice in creative writing.

B. Materials: Pencils, paper, and a selection of novels which have their settings in other countries.

C. Introduction and Procedures: Each student is to read a novel and pretend to be an exchange student living in that country. They are instructed to write a letter to their parents or a friend. This letter should consist of impressions or facts about the country in which they are living, as well as tell how they are feeling living away from home.

45. Write an Ending (Grades 3-8)

A. Purpose: To promote higher order thinking and develop composition skills.

B. Materials: A mystery story, paper, and pencils.

C. Introduction and Procedures: The teacher should select a fairly short mystery story to read to the class. The teacher should read the story aloud up to the point in the plot where the foundation has been laid, and suspense created, but anything can happen. The students are instructed to write the ending. These endings should be shared with the class. The class should then vote on the best ending. Then the teacher should read the actual ending of the story from the book.

46. Create a Newspaper (Grades 3-8)

A. Purpose: To develop expository writing skills.

B. Materials: Paper and pencils; The entire class needs to have read a particular book prior to this activity.

C. Introduction and Procedures: The children are to create a newspaper using the main topic or ideas from the book that all the students read. The newspaper might contain editorials, weather reports, feature stories, historical events, advertisements, drawings, or just about anything one might see in a newspaper. In feature stories, a student can pretend to be the main character or take the part of the protagonist or antagonist of the story. If the book read was a historical one, the newspaper is beneficial because it gives a variety of experiences in writing of different types. It also helps students understand a story better by looking at it from another person's point of view.

Zoo to Spruce Up Its Elephant House:
Ruth, Kita to Get New Pool
by James L. Kerwin

Among the oldest tenants of the Detroit Zoo, elephants Ruth and Kita finally are getting some respect from their landlord. Their quarters, which date back to the early 1930's, are in shambles. The interior is drab and dreary. Exterior walls made from granite are peeling away. The roof leaks, the plumbing leaves them standing in smelly water, and new electrical wiring is needed. Conditions are so bad they can't even have visitors from among the thousands who drop by the zoo each day to view the wildlife exhibits. But a major renovation has begun to correct the deficiencies, and add a few new features— improved landscaping, a flight cage with exotic birds to keep company with the aging pachyderms, new display graphics that tells visitors all about Asian elephants and an indoor pool to help them keep tidy and cool.

47. Biographies (Grades 3-8)

A. Purpose: To assist students' in learning how to write biographies.

B. Materials: Crayons, pencils, cardboard, and old magazines.

C. Introduction and Procedures: Provide a table in the room to display the above mentioned materials. Each student must select a partner with whom to work. Each partner is to interview the other and then write a biography of his/her partner. Using the materials listed above, each partner will construct a book. The cardboard serves as a book cover and the old magazines can provide illustrations. Illustrations could also be done with pencils and crayons. The biographies should be shared with the class.

48. Complete a Story (Grades 3-8)

A. Purpose: To develop the students' creative writing skills.

B. Materials: A selection of short stories, paper, and pencils.

C. Introduction and Procedures: Choose a short story to read to the students. Read the first part of the story to them. Stop at a point when they seem to be well involved in the plot. They are then instructed to finish the story. This could also be done by reading the <u>last half</u> of the story and asking them to write the beginning.

49. Story Variations (Grades 3-8)

A. Purpose: To provide practice in creative writing.

B. Materials: *Nothing Ever Happens On My Block*, by Ellen Raskin, pencils, paper, and markers.

C. Introduction and Procedures: Read the book to the class. Talk about the characters and the setting. Divide the class into groups of six. One member of each group draws a slip of paper out of a box. On the slips of paper, one of the following should have been written:

> 1. Change the title so it fits the title, Nothing Ever Happens On My Farm.
>
> 2. Change the story so it fits the title, Nothing Ever Happens On My Zoo.
>
> 3. Change the story so it fits the title, Nothing Ever Happens In My School.
>
> 4. Change the story using an elephant to tell the story.
>
> 5. Change the story using a kitten to tell the story. (Any animal can be used).

6. Change the story, using the current United States President to tell the story.

7. Change the story, using George Washington to tell the story. (Any famous person can be used).

Have the groups share their newly-written stories with the class.

50. Create a Power Point Story (Grades 3-8)

A. Purpose: To develop the students' creative thinking skills.

B. Materials: Power Point stories, an In-Focus projector, computer with Power Point.

C. Introduction and Procedures: The students should be shown several Power Point slide show stories. The teacher guides students through the process of creating a slide show. Students are then asked, individually or in groups, to write and illustrate (may use clip art) their own stories. The students then present their stories to the class and discuss possible improvements.

51. Riddle Box (Grades K-5)

A. Purpose: To promote understanding of main idea and promote interest in reading.

B. Materials: A large box, short stories, and children books.

C. Introduction and Procedures: Cut the top off a large box and decorate it. This becomes the riddle box as students create riddles about stories read in class. The riddle might describe the book and ask for the title, or describe a character in it and ask for the character's name. An example might be, "I am a book about a boy who becomes friends with a dinosaur," or "I rode on a dinosaur's back. Who am I?" Answers: *Danny and the Dinosaur*, Danny. With primary children, this is teacher-directed.

52. Visual Book Reporting (Grades 3-8)

A. Purpose: To promote creative thinking by responding to literature in a different way.

B. Materials: Novels, magazines, newspapers, scissors, markers, glue, poster board, index cards.

C. Introduction and Procedures: This is a creative form of book reporting. Students are to cut pictures from magazines and newspapers that depict an idea, the items, or an actual scene from the novel they have read. The pictures are to be glued to poster board, leaving a large border around them. On this border, the students are to arrange words or phrases the explain or describe the story. They are instructed to look for vivid adjectives and verbs. On the back of the poster board, they are to attach an index card which should contain the title, author, and a brief summary of the book.

53. Mobiles (Grades 3-8)

A. Purpose: To develop a sense of story.

B. Materials: Construction paper, newspaper, two dowels, heavy string.

C. Introduction and Procedures: Mobiles depicting stories read are created and hung from the ceiling. This can be done in groups or individually. To create a mobile, lay the two sticks an a + and tie the two sticks together where they cross. Then add the string through the tip of the objects being used and attach the other end of the strings to the sticks.

54. Name the Chapters (3-8)

A. Purpose: To develop understanding of the main idea.

B. Materials: A selection of novels.

C. Introduction and Procedures: This activity is best introduced with a class set of the same novel. As each chapter is finished, have the class brainstorm the main events of the chapter and decide on a good title. A table of contents is created as each chapter is given a title.

Unit 8

Interdisciplinary Curricular Connections

Current research indicates that interdisciplinary instruction will facilitate comprehension. (Kellough, 1999). Many teachers have successfully managed to integrate reading and writing across the curriculum. These teachers reflect current beliefs that learning and literacy development is a social and constructive process, that language is best learned when used for authentic, meaningful purposes (Cox, 2001). This section presents creative approaches to elementary curriculum, with an emphasis on the use of technology. Our changing society demands an emphasis on raising student awareness of the role of technology. Unit VII includes a variety of lesson activities which integrate the teaching of science, math and social studies to the teaching of language arts. For example, graphs and charts can be created on the computer which assist students in clearly showing the results of data analysis in the subjects of science and mathematics. Having students write descriptive narrative about the graphs and charts extends the subject matter into the language arts. Students can also take measurements and record observational data which then become the data for drawing conclusions and predicting further outcomes based on the charts and graphs.

Interdisciplinary Curricular Connections
Activities

1. **Pretend to be an animal: Keeping a Diary (Grades 3-8)**

   A. Purpose: To develop higher order thinking skills and composition.

   B. Materials: A selection of non-fiction books about animals, paper and pencils.

   C. Introduction and Procedures: The students are instructed to read about a particular animal, habitat, enemies, and the food it eats. Students are to then write a diary entry, or a day in the life of their animal.

2. **Weather/Poetry/Cinquain (All grade levels, Teacher directed, primary students)**

   A. Purpose: To develop creative thinking and composition skills.

   B. Materials: A selection of children's books.

   C. Introduction and Procedures: Explain the structure of a cinquain poem, doing some examples with the students. Write the structure on the board. Students are to write a cinquain about a story element in the children's book read (this can be about the character. The cinquain works well with setting.

   Title . . . . snow

   Describe the title . . . . cold, white

   Action, action, action . . . . falling, chilling, stopping

   Feeling about the title . . . . people stay at home

   Title . . . . snow

3. Night and Day/Earth's rotation/Poetry/Diamante (All grades, Teacher directed, primary students)

A. Purpose: To develop creative thinking and composition skills.

B. Materials: A selection of children's books.

C. Introduction and Procedures: Explain the structure of the diamante poem, doing some examples on the board.

noun . . . . night

two adjectives . . . . dark, black

three participles . . . . sleeping, dreaming, relaxing

four nouns or a phrase . . . . nobody is moving

three participles noting change . . . yawning, stretching, standing

2 adjectives . . . . bright sunny

contrasting noun . . . . daylight

Other examples of contrasting nouns: solid/liquid; plant/animal; hot/cold; summer/winter.

4. Discover My Category (Grades 3-8)

A. Purpose: To develop vocabulary and provide practice in classification.

B. Materials: A selection of children's books, paper and pencils.

C. Introduction and Procedures: The students are instructed to read their book looking for words which specifically focus on a particular category or classification. They are to divide their papers into a a number of sections as follows: (Other categories can be added)

Animal	Plant	Rock	Plastic	Metal	?	?
dog cat	lilac lily	granite quartz	comb disk	Gold Tin		

The sensory words are placed in the appropriate columns. The student chooses a partner to share his/her list of words and the partner is to write a story using as many of these words as possible.

5. Landforms and Organisms/Poetry for Science (Grades 3-8)

A   Purpose: To extend poetry into science learning experiences.

B. Materials: Samples of various poetry forms, poetry books.

C. Introduction and Procedures: Students will be asked to express science information through various forms of poetry. A landform, organism, or other science concept can become a haiku, cinquain, diamante, free verse, concrete, or acrostic. These poems could then be shared with the class.

Acrostic (Mesa)	Diamante—Night & Day	
	Diamante Poem format:	Sample diamante:
Mound	noun:	night
Elevated	two adjectives:	dark, black
Sleep-sloped	three participles:	sleeping, dreaming, relaxing
Area	four nouns or a phrase:	nobody is moving
	three participles noting change:	yawning, stretching, standing
	two adjectives	bright, sunny
	contrary noun	daylight

Cinquain—Molting	
Cinquain poem format:	Sample Cinquain:
Line 1: a one-word subject with two syllables	molting
Line 2: four syllables describing the subject	scaly, dry
Line 3: six syllables showing action	itchy, flaky, crispy
Line 4: eight syllables expressing a feeling of observation about the subject	trying hard to get rid of it
Line 5: two syllables describing and renaming the subject	growing

6. Autobiography/Timelines (Grades 3-8)

A. Purpose: To provide experiences with creative writing.

B. Materials: A selection of autobiographies, of varying readability levels, paper and pencils.

C. Introduction and Procedures: To introduce the idea of autobiography, students will develop a timeline depicting the major events in their lives. Then, as they read their selected autobiography, they will complete a timeline depicting the major events in their lives, Then, as they read their selected autobiography, they will complete a timeline   on the famous person.

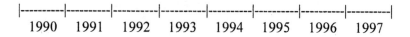

|----------|----------|----------|----------|----------|----------|----------|----------|
1990   1991   1992   1993   1994   1995   1996   1997

Upon completion of the timeline, students will select one event to develop into a composition. Timelines can also be developed as a response to reading a fiction story, or a   non-fiction selection showing the history or life cycle of something.

7. Rewrite the Titles (Grades 3-8)

A. Purpose: To develop composition skill and use of thesauri across the curriculum.

B. Materials: Thesaurus, selection of children's literature.

C. Introduction and Procedures: The teacher writes the titles of a selection of children's books on the board, underlining key terms. In groups of four, students are to look up the underlined words in the thesaurus and reword the titles of the books:

Examples:

The <u>teacher</u> from
    the <u>Black Lagoon</u>   The instructor from the Neon Bayou

Little Women   Tiny Ladies

Other subjects:

"<u>Honest</u> Abe"	Truth-telling Abe
"We <u>Like</u> Ike"	We vote for Ike
"<u>Big Bad</u> John"	Tall Ugly John

8. Grocery Lists (Grades 2-5)

A. Purpose: To develop creative thinking skills.

B. Materials: A selection of picture books, grocery ads from local newspapers.

C. Introduction and Procedures: This activity can be done individually in groups of four or with the total class. After the book is read, students are to think about the characters in the story they read, and pretend they are going to the store to buy groceries for one week. They are to create a grocery list. An excellent interdisciplinary extension would have them plan balanced meals using foods from their grocery list.

9. Fractured Folk Tales (Grades 3-8)

A. Purpose: To develop higher order thinking skills and composition skills.

B. Materials: A selection of books containing fairy tales, paper and pencils.

C. Introduction and Procedures: Each group of four reads a familiar folk tale and makes a list of the characters in the story. Two groups meet together and give one of their characters to the other group to include in their story. (i.e., put Abe Lincoln into Johnnie Appleseed). They re-write the folk tale changing it to include the new character. Or put George Washington into Pinocchio.

Character—Folktakes	Common Themes	Sample
Abe Lincoln Johnny Appleseed	Country boy Walked about Served as examples Hero reputations	Abe met Johnny when Johnny was on his way through Illinois planting his Apple trees, etc.
George Washington Pinocchio	Truth or lies Consequences Wooden teeth	George was the truth poster boy; "I cannot tell a lie." Pinocchio on the other hand got famous for lies and his nose grew. Together they traveled around to schools, telling children of the consequences, etc.

10. Join the Story (Grades 3-8)

A. Purpose: Narrative writing in the first person.

B. Materials: A selection of novels with varying reading levels, paper and pencils.

C. Introduction and Procedures: Following the reading of a passage or book about a famous person in American History, students are to choose their favorite event and rewrite that event adding themselves as a character and writing in the first person. (Note: This process should be demonstrated as a class before having students attempt to do it independently. A short story can be used effectively in a group situation.)

Sample: <u>Washington crossing the Delaware</u>:

"I felt cold as the boat banged and bumped into the pieces of ice. I wanted so bad to be noticed by General Washington. It would be nice to have him ask me my name. However, before

I could think of a way to get his attention, the boat shifted and he fell on top of me. I was a hero. I saved General Washington from bumping his head when he fell."

11. Folk Heroes/Poetry/Limericks (All grades, Teacher directed, primary students)

A. Purpose: To develop creative thinking and encourage language development.

B. Materials: A selection of short stories or children's books.

C. Introduction and Procedures: Read aloud several examples of limericks, emphasizing the structure of the poem. Write an example on the board, with the structure:

There was a dog named . . . .

Line 1 _____ a
                                   rhyme
Line 2 _____ a

Line 3 _____ b
                                   rhyme
Line 4 _____ b

Line 5 _____ a

Although limericks are supposed to be silly and just for fun, they can be used to assist students in retaining difficult content information. Students are to write a limerick about the main character in their children's book. This is fun in groups of four.

12. Let's Plan a Trip (Grades 3-8)

A. Purpose: To improve comprehension and business letter writing.

B. Materials: A selection of picture books or short stories, paper and pencils.

C. Introduction and Procedures: Each child should read a short story or picture book with setting somewhere in the United States. The teacher then should write a sample business letter on the chalkboard. This letter should request information on a particular location. Each child will write to the Chamber of Commerce of the capital city of the state which is the setting of his/her book. When the brochures arrive, the children should share them with the class, and then create a persuasive tourist brochure convincing the class to visit the location.

13. The Five Senses Game (Grades 2-5)

A. Purpose: To improve students' ability to describe.

B. Materials: Ordinary objects; a worm, a piece of bark, a leaf, a mud puddle, a brick wall, etc.

C.Introduction and Procedures: By providing objects for students to describe and then focusing on one sense (smell), students are asked to describe the object presented. The teacher tries to draw out descriptive terms related to texture, feel, and touch. The same thing can be done with the other senses: sight, hearing, smell, and taste. (The teacher may want to ensure that tasting be done only with things that he/she brought to the classroom.)

Red Rose				
Taste	Smell	Hearing	Sight	Touch
xxxxxxxxx	sweet odor, increases as rose is opened	Roses make an interesting sound when a bouquet of roses is carried.	beautiful, red, green	silky blossom, sharp thorns, many petals

14. The Observation Game (Grades 1-8)

A. Purpose: To improve students' ability to describe, develop visual memory.

B. Materials: The cover of a picture book or a picture from history, series of questions that relate to the picture.

C. Introduction and Procedures: Provide students with a cover from a picture book or picture from history (or a tray covered with objects), the era being studied, and allow students to look at it for 30 seconds. The teacher then asks students questions related to the picture such as:

1. How many people were there in the picture?

2. What was the woman in the picture doing?

3. Were there both men and woman in the picture?

4. What was the child doing in the picture?

5. What type of plants were growing in the picture?

6. What was the weather like in the picture?

Then read the book to the students and show the pictures.

15. What Kind of Book Do You Like? (Grades 1-5)

A. Purpose: To help students learn to read a graph or table.

B. Materials: Provide a picture book dealing with sports, a picture book dealing with animals, a fairy tale, and a science story. (These subjects can be changed to fit the needs of the group.)

C. Introduction and Procedures: The teacher draws the following table on the chalkboard.

		xxxxxxxxxxxx xxxxxxxxxxxx	
		xxxxxxxxxxxx xxxxxxxxxxxx	xxxxxxxxxxx xxxxxxxxxxx
xxxxxxxxxxx xxxxxxxxxxx	xxxxxxxxxxxx xxxxxxxxxxxx	xxxxxxxxxxxx xxxxxxxxxxxx	xxxxxxxxxxx xxxxxxxxxxx
sports	animals	fair tale	science

The teacher now reads a short story on each of the topics used. The children are to color a box above the book they like best. When the table is completed have the following questions answered in class discussion:

1. How many children are in the class?

2. Which kind of book was liked the most?

3. Which kind of book was liked the least?

16. Reading a Table (Grades 3-5)

A. Purpose: To gain information from a table.

B. aterials: A selection of picture books.

C. Introduction and Procedures: The teacher should write the following table on the chalkboard:

		XXXXXXXXXXX XXXXXXXXXXX	
	XXXXXXXXXXX XXXXXXXXXXX	XXXXXXXXXXX XXXXXXXXXXX	XXXXXXXXXXX XXXXXXXXXXX
XXXXXXXXXXX XXXXXXXXXXX	XXXXXXXXXXX XXXXXXXXXXX	XXXXXXXXXXX XXXXXXXXXXX	XXXXXXXXXXX XXXXXXXXXXX
sad	happy	scary	funny

The children are to read a picture book, decide whether it is sad, happy, scary, or funny and color in one box over the appropriate word. When this is completed, the group should answer the following questions:

1. How many books were read in all?
2. Which kind of book was read the most?
3. Which kind of book was read the least?

17. That's My Line? (Grades 2-5)

A. Purpose: To arouse student's interest in various books.

B. Materials: Several copies of five different library books.

C. Introduction and Procedures: At the beginning of the week, the teacher gives a short introduction of the books to arouse interest. The students are instructed to read each of the books before Friday. The topics of the books should be similar. (For example, all about outer space adventures) On Friday, after everyone has had a chance to read the books, pick five students from the class to play "What's My Line?" One of the five students is chosen to be "it" and selects a character from one of the books to portray. The panel can only ask "yes" or "no" questions to determine who the person is portraying and what book he/she is from. Each panel member asks one question at a time and the panel has ten guesses to determine the character. The student who identifies the correct character gets to select the next character to portray.

18. Tic-Tac-Toe (Grades 3-6)

A. Purpose: To create interest in reading library (fiction or non-fiction) books.

B. Materials: Provide a tic-tac-toe game board such as the one below.

C. Introduction and Procedures: Each child should have read all nine of the stories on the tic-tac-toe game board before attempting to play the game. The class writes questions about each story on slips of paper. The papers are put into an envelope, using one envelope for each story. Two children play the game. The players draw a question from the envelope of the story of their choice. If answered correctly, the player puts either an "X" or "O" over the appropriate square. The game continues until the "X," the "O" or the "Ole Cat" (a tie) wins.

The books in the squares are rotated to match the topics being covered in the subjects of history, science, and social studies.

whales	train to nowhere	two bad ants
butterfly seeds	grandfather's journey	just a dream
Nettie's trip south	tin heart	verdi

19. Non-Fiction Books (Grades 3-8)

A. Purpose: To give students opportunities to read non-fiction.

B. Materials: A selection of non-fiction, informational books, poster board, pencils and markers.

C. Introduction and Procedures: Students are instructed to read their informational book and make a poster listing six facts learned from each book. The posters can be displayed around the room. Each student is asked to share the poster orally with the group, giving the author, title, the main idea the author wanted to get across and discussing the six facts learned.

20. Riddles (Grades 2-5)

A. Purpose: To enhance reading comprehension (including content subjects).

B. Materials: Several books dealing with riddles, paper and pencils.

C. Introduction and Procedures: The teacher should read some "What Am I?" riddles to the class. Divide the class into groups of four or five. Each group is to come up with some riddles to stump the class. The younger children will probably need to use the riddle books, while the other ones will write some of their own.

21. Let's Classify (Grades 3-6)

A. Purpose: To learn how to classify books.

B. Materials: Provide fifty 3x5 cards of one color, six 3x5 cards of another color, a marking pen and poster board for constructing game boards.

C. Introduction and Procedures: Each student should construct a board which contains 12 pockets. Print the title of a book on each of the fifty cards of one color. On the six cards of another color, print these categories: Science, Biography, Humor or Fairy Tales, Sports, Science Fiction and Myths or Legends. The title cards are shuffled and dealt to each player until all of the pockets of everyone's board is filled. The students take turns drawing a category card. Then he/she remove from the pockets those titles of books which belong in that category. He/she replaces the category card to the bottom of the pile. (Example: If a child draws the category card

"Biography," he may remove all stories about the lives of people.) The game ends when one player removes all his/her cards.

22. What Season Is It? (Grades K-4)

A. Purpose: To categorize through reading comprehension.

B. Materials: A selection of picture books.

C. Introduction and Procedures: The teacher should write the following headings on the chalkboard:

Autumn	Winter	Spring	Summer

Each child reads a picture book and places the title of the story under the season in which the story takes place. When everyone is through, the children should share something about their books, telling why they believe the story took place in that season.

23. Let's Categorize (Grades 3-5)

A. Purpose: To assist students in learning to classify.

B. Materials: Provide a selection of non-fiction books dealing with the main topic (example: foods), paper and pencils.

C. Introduction and Procedures: Two students will work together in this activity. They are given one book and are instructed to find words to place under the proper heading. Using books dealing with food, the following categories might be used:

1. Cereal and Breads

2. Meats

3. Vegetables and Fruits

4. Milk and Dairy

The categories can be changed to fit information on any topic.

24. Categories (Grades 2-4)

A. Purpose: To teach children to categorize; a precursor to main idea.

B. Materials: Paper, pencils, and numerous picture books for choice.

C. Introduction and Procedures: Discuss groups of things with the class. Use a sample category to make a list on the chalkboard (examples: nouns, foods). Read a picture book to the students. Divide a section of the chalkboard into three pieces. Write the following headings at the top of the board:

People	Places	Things

As a group, complete the chart on the chalkboard. Give each student a picture book to read and have him do the above exercise independently. The categories can be changed to fit the books used.

25. Anticipation Guide (Grades 2-5)

A. Purpose: To practice prediction and verification activities.

B. Materials: Anticipation guide for *Sylvester and the Magic Pebble*, by William Steig.

C. Introduction and Procedures: Give each student a copy of the anticipation guide for *Sylvester and the Magic Pebble,* and have them write yes or no before each statement as a prediction of whether the statement is true. Then read the book. Finally, have students write yes or no after the statements based on the book. Then have students compare their answers to see how many statements they had correct.

Anticipation Guide for *Sylvester and the Magic Pebble*, by William Steig.

Write Yes or No before each statement:

_____1. Sylvester lived with his parents._____

_____2. Sylvester left his parents when he was old enough to get job._____

_____3. Sylvester was eaten by a lion._____

_____4. Sylvester spent a year as a pebble._____

_____5. Sylvester had to remain a pebble the rest of his life._____

After reading the book, write Yes or No after each statement. Compare your answers. *Sylvester and the Magic Pebble* has many aspects that relate to content subjects.

Examples: Seasonal changes during the year, family values, community searches, emotions and feelings.

26. Goldilocks and the Three Bears (Grades K-1)

A. Purpose: Teach students the need for rules and laws.

B. Materials: *Goldilocks and the Three Bears*, paper plates, and tongue depressors.

C. Introduction and Procedures: While listening to *Goldilocks and the Three Bears*, students are asked to show either the happy face or the sad face they have made on their paper plate (attached to a tongue depressor for a handle) to tell whether what Goldilocks is doing is either sad or happy. After the story, discuss what Goldilocks did that was wrong and why it is wrong.

27. Rock and Roll—Multiple Intelligences (Grades 4-8)

A. Purpose: To offer student selection of activity to learn about rocks.

B. Materials: Rock collection, *Everybody Needs a Rock*, by Byrd Baylor, rocks and minerals reference book, dictionary.

C. Introduction and Procedures: Students will be asked to choose two of the following:

1. Verbal/Linguistic: brainstorm rock words and illustrate a rock dictionary.

2. Logical/Mathematical: pretend to be a geologist being interviewed; distinguish between igneous and sedimentary rocks.

3. Visual/Spatial: draw an outline map of the US and mark & label the locations where ten rocks or minerals would be found.

4. Body/Kinesthetic: design ten different "rocks and minerals" trivia cards.

5. Musical/Rhythmic: make up "rock and roll" songs and sign them while silent filmstrips are rolled (drawn on adding machine tapes or shelf paper rolls).

6. Interpersonal: work with a friend to research some unusual rock formation and prepare a fold-out presentation to share your findings.

7. Intrapersonal: give reasons why you would like to be a geologist or a gemologist.

28. Weathering the Weather—Multiple Intelligences (Grades 4-8)

A. Purpose: To offer student selection of activity to learn about weather.

B. Materials: Weather reports, *Thundercake*, by Patricia Polacco, weather reference book, dictionary.

C. Introduction and Procedures: Students will be asked to choose two of the following:

   1. Verbal/Linguistic: read several myths or legends and then write an original myth using real weather terms, concepts, and conditions in tell the story.

   2. Logical/Mathematical: pretend to be a meteorologist being interviewed; distinguish between a cold front and an warm front or similar conditions.

   3. Visual/Spatial: draw an outline map of the US and turn it into a collage of as many weather conditions as you can find. Write a one page summary of the collage.

   4. Body/Kinesthetic: cut the weather maps out of the newspaper for five consecutive days and create a presentation entitled, "Our Weather This Week."

   5. Musical/Rhythmic: research some rain dances and create an original dance routine of your own.

   6. Interpersonal: stage a debate between Summer and Winter, using elements of weather to determine the content of the debate.

   7. Intrapersonal: write a short essay on how you feel about the weather in your local area.

29. Collecting the Shells (Grades 3-8)

A. Purpose: To facilitate student understanding of Williams Taxonomy using shells.

B. Materials: Shell collection, *Is This a Home for Hermit Crab,* by Eric Carle, shell reference book, dictionary.

C. Introduction and Procedures: Students will work in groups to do the following:

    1. Fluency: List as many types of shells as you can.

    2. Flexibility: Classify your list according to the uses that could be made of these different types.

    3. Originality: Create a wallpaper, stationery, or wrapping paper design using a shell motif.

    4. Elaboration: What kinds of characteristics of a living animal can you infer from examining its shell after the animal is gone?

    5. Risk Taking: Tell how you feel about people who pick up shells in protected areas where collecting shells is prohibited.

    6. Complexity: Think of some ways to compare the hermit crab to some human beings. Use similes, metaphors, or other descriptive language.

    7. Curiosity: Pretend you are interviewing a zoologist who specializes in animals that grow shells. What questions would you ask to learn more about these animals?

    8. Imagination: Design a unique and effective way to organize a collection of shells   for display.

30. Graphing Your Favorites (Grades 2-8)

A. Purpose: Conduct individual or group surveys and show results in chart form.

B. Materials: Graphs.

C. Introduction and Procedures: Students will brainstorm survey ideas, conduct surveys, and graph their results. Students could graph the number of boys and girls, favorite literature genre, favorite colors, favorite school subject, favorite pets, favorite sport or TV show, etc.

31. Music in My Science Ears (Grades K-5)

A. Purpose: To extend music into science learning experiences.

B. Materials: Samples of various music forms, music books.

C. Introduction and Procedures: Students will be asked to create science songs to the of familiar songs. A plant may become a song, sung to the tune of "Did You Ever See a Lassie Go This Way and That Way."

> Have you ever seen a flower, a flower, a flower?
> Have you ever seen a flower as wonderful as me?
> > With strong roots and a long stem
> > With large leaves and colored petals
> Have you ever seen a flower, a flower, a flower?
> Have you ever seen a flower as wonder as me?
> > I drink water with my roots
> > It travels up my long, long stem
> > From the stem it travels on ward
> > To my leaves and then my head
> Have you ever seen a flower, a flower, a flower?
> Have you ever seen a flower as wonderful as me?

32. Picture Books for Science (Grades 3-8)

A. Purpose: To add to student knowledge of science concepts; to extend science reading to other genres and resources; fiction and non-fiction.

B. Materials: Collection of children's books on science topics being studied.

C. Introduction and Procedures: Students will read a variety of books on science topics, on a variety of levels, including a variety of resources such as internet sites which include sound, video, and virtual fieldtrips.

33. Rubbings and Observation (Grades K-5)

A. Purpose: Increase awareness of texture of living things.

B. Materials: A variety of leaves, bark, and plant fibers. C. Introduction to the Class: Students take ordinary paper and place it over leaves, bark, and other plant fibers and rub with crayons to create "rubbings" that clearly show lines, patterns, and structures found on plants.

34. Create a Category Game (Grades 1-8)

A. Purpose: To increase students' ability to recognize a category; classify.

B. Materials: Rocks, buttons, seeds, or other multi-colored, multi-attribute objects, *The Memory String*, by Eve Bunting. C. Introduction and Procedures: Students will listen to *The Memory String* by Eve Bunting. Each bead on the string a special meaning. Students will create a memory string of their own by stringing buttons that remind them of significant events from their lives. Student will also play "Create a Category." Given any bunch of objects, students will create categories to sort the objects into whether the objects are rocks or buttons or seeds. Objects can be sorted by color, size, number of holes, or other attribute or characteristic. Students then explain their categories.

35. Science Reader's Theatre (3-8)

A. Purpose: To increase student knowledge of science topics being studied.

B. Materials: Scripts that relate to science topics being studied. (Ex. *Joyful Noise*).

C. Introduction and Procedures: Students will be given scripts to be used in presenting science reader's theatre. Scripts can be created by the teacher or with student input as research skills develop. One of the excerpts has two insects talking to each other, professing their love and talking about their future.

36. Pyramiding into Science (Grades 3-8)

A. Purpose: To increase student knowledge of science content through poetry forms.

B. Materials: A selection of children's books on topics to be covered in science and also children's books illustrating poetry forms.

C. Introduction and Procedures: Students will be asked to choose a poetry form and then create a poem focused on a science topic being studied.

37. Poetry in Science (Grades 3-8)

A. Purpose: To increase student knowledge of science content through poetry forms.

B. Materials: Children's books illustrating samples of poetry forms.

C. Introduction and Procedures: Students will choose to create a pyramid, concrete, haiku, diamante, or other type of poem using their science content vocabulary. Example: After reviewing poetry forms, students will read about a topic and discuss it in groups. Students will then create poetry forms using science information.

38. Columbus Reader's Theatre for Social Studies (Grades 3-8)

A. Purpose: To increase student understanding of the early explorers.

B. Materials: Reader's Theatre script on a segment of adventures of Columbus.

C. Introduction and Procedures: After students have studied Columbus and his adventures, students will each be assisted in writing a script of an adventure of Columbus and will perform the script with little or no rehearsal. Sample Script:

> Columbus: "Land ho! Let's go meet the Indians."
>
> First Mate: "But sir! This is not India! Let's move on and not bother these people."
>
> Columbus: "What could it hurt?"
>
> (Etc.)

39. Talking Science Drawings (Grades 2-8)

A. Purpose: To diagnosis and then increase student knowledge of topics in science.

B. Materials: Children's books on science topics—fiction and non-fiction.

C. Introduction and Procedures: Students will be asked to draw pictures illustrating their present knowledge of selected topics in science. After reading and researching the same topics, students will then add to their drawings illustrating increased knowledge.

40. Pantomiming Organism Behavior in Science (Grades 2-8)

A. Purpose: To diagnose and then increase student knowledge of organisms in science

B. Materials: Children's books on science topics—fiction and non-fiction

C. Introduction and Procedures: Students will be asked to imitate or pantomime the behavior of an organism. Students will then read and research the organism. Students will make a second attempt at imitating the behavior of the organism based on increased knowledge and information.

41. Cubing up Science (Grades 3-8)

A. Purpose: To increase student knowledge of science topics and composition skills.

B. Materials: Explanation of cubing, children's books.

C. Introduction and Procedures: Students will be given a concept and a cube with the words: describe, compare, associate, analyze, apply, and argue. Using their science concept they will then describe it (the process, event, features, traits), compare it (similar to or different from?), associate it (analogies, make me think of?), analyze it (composed of? steps, procedures?), apply it (how can it be applied to other situations?), and argue for or against it (support your position).

Concepts to be used with the cube:

  Math—congruence, transformations

  Science—photosynthesis, mitosis

  Social Studies—democracy, tolerance, compromise

42. K-W-L-Plus in Science (Grades 2-8)

A. Purpose: To increase reading comprehension through the use of brainstorming, purpose-setting, reflecting, and organizing information.

B. Materials: An appropriate science passage or text.

C. Introduction and Procedures: Students will use the K-W-L chart to carry out three phases of the process. First, they will brainstorm what they know about the topic (K), then they will list what they want to know (W), then list what I learned (L), finally summarizing the chart by drawing a semantic map to use in creating a written summary (Plus).

What we Know	What We Want to Know	What We Learned	Plus (Summarize)
Orcas are seen in movies. Orcas eat seals.	What happened to Willy? What else do orcas eat?	Orcas also eat other animals. Willy has been moved and is still alive.	The orcas seen on TV eat seals and other animals. Willy has a new home and is still alive.

43. Imagine, Elaborate, Predict, and Confirm Chart and Science (Grades 3-8)

A. Purpose: To increase student understanding and recall by using visual imagery to predict events in a selection.

B. Materials: IEPC chart show below; passage appropriate for developing imagery on science topics being studied, fiction and non-fiction.

C. Introduction and Procedures: The teacher will model the four processes using the think-aloud approach: imagine (I), elaborate

(E), predict (P), and confirm (C) using a science text passage. Then students will carry out the same processes: Imagine: Students will first —close their eyes and try to imagine the scene, then share their ideas with a partner and the whole class. Elaborate: Then students think of details surrounding the scene in their head. How do you think the characters feel? What are similar experiences? Describe the scene. What do you see, feel, hear, smell? Predict: Use what you have imagined in your head to predict what might happen in the story (characters, events, setting, etc.); Confirm: During and after reading the selection, think about your original predictions. Were they true, false, or were they not explained in the passage? Modify your predictions to coordinate with the actual selection.

Imagine	Elaborate	Predict	Confirm

44. Oobleck? (Grade 2-5)

A. Purpose: To increase student understanding of integrating curriculum.

B. Materials: "Oobleck" (made with corn starch and water), Bartholomew and the Oobleck, by Dr. Seuss, handout listing tests to be made on the oobleck, data chart, pie graph.

C Introduction and Procedures: Corn starch and water need to be mixed to create "oobleck," which can be dyed with food coloring to match the color in the book. The book should be read to the students. A review of the properties of liquids and solids needs to be carried out with the students. Groups of students need to be given a cup with "oobleck" in it. It should be wet enough to be somewhat runny, yet still have some consistency. Students then are asked to perform tests on the "oobleck," recording whether the substance performed like a liquid or a solid. After doing a slow-poke finger test, a quick-poke finger test, a bounce test, a heat test (using a candle), a conforming to the container test, a pounding test, etc. the student then tabulates the totals to see if the substance performs more like a solid or a liquid. The test data is used to color the pie graph to visually display whether the group of students decides the "oobleck" is a liquid or a solid. Further study can include looking at the properties of colloids.

REFERENCES

Anderson, R.C., & Freebody, P. (1981). Vocabulary knowledge, In *Comprehension and Teaching: Research Reviews*, ed. J. Guthrie, 77-117. Newark, DE: International Reading Association.

Bradley, K.S. (1987). *Kid's lit*. Stevensville, Michigan: Education Service Inc.

Cox, C. (2002). *Teaching language arts: A Student-and response-centered classroom* (4th ed.). Boston: Allyn & Bacon.

Graves, M.F., Juel, C., & Graves, B.B. (2001). *Teaching reading in the 21st century (2nd ed.)*. Needham Height, MA: Allyn & Bacon.

Gunning, T.G. (2000). *Phonological awareness and primary phonics*. Boston: Allyn and Bacon.

Gunning, T.G. (2003). *Creating literacy instruction for all children* (4th ed.). Boston: Allyn & Bacon.

Harris, T., & Hodges, R. (eds.). (1995). *The literacy dictionary*. Newark, DE: International Reading Association.

Heilman, A.W., Blair, T.R., & Rupley, W.H. (2002). *Principles and practices in the teaching of reading* (10th ed.). Upper Saddle River, N.J.: Merrill.

Kellough, R.D., & Kellough, N.G. (1999). *Middle school teaching: A guide to methods and resources* (3rd ed.). Upper Saddle River, N.J.: Prentice-Hall.
Nagy, W. (1988). *Teaching vocabulary to improve reading comprehension*. Newark, DE: International Reading Association.

Pearson, D. (2001). *Focus on research: Teaching and learning reading: A research perspective.* Language Arts, 70(6), 502-511.

Robinson, R., McKenna, M., & Wedman, J. (2000). *Issues and trends in literacy education.* Needham Heights, MA: Allyn and Bacon.

Ruddell, R.B. (2002). *Teaching children to read and write: Becoming an effective literacy teacher* (3rd ed.). Boston: Allyn & Bacon.

Salinger, T. (1996). *Literacy for young children* (2nd ed.). Englewood Cliffs, N.J.: Merrill.

Shanker, J.L. & Ekwall, E.E. (2003). *Locating and correcting reading difficulties.* (8th ed.). Upper Saddle River, N.J.: Prentice-Hall.

Snow, C., Griffin, P., & Burns, S. (1999). *Starting out right.* Washington D.C.: National Academy Press.

Tompkins, G. (2003). *Literacy for the 21st Century (3rd ed.).* Upper Saddle River, NJ: Prentice-Hall.

Vacca, J.L., Vacca, R.T., Gove, M.K., Burkey, L., Lenhart, L.A., & McKeon, C. (2003). *Reading and Learning to Read* (5th ed.). Boston: Allyn & Bacon.

Wood, K.D. & Harmon, J.M. (2001). *Strategies for integrating reading & writing in middle and high school classrooms.* Westerville, OH: Nation Middle School Association.

Wynn, M.J. (1996). *Creative teaching strategies: A resource book for K-8.* Albany, NY: Delmar.

INDEX